THE ULTIMATUM

THE ULTIMATUM

Does the Qur'an Command
Killing Non-Muslims?

Ahmet Kurucan

BLUE DOME

ISBN: 978-1-68206-034-6
Ebook: 978-1-68206-541-9

Published by Blue Dome Press
335 Clifton Ave.
Clifton, NJ, 07011, USA
www.tughrabooks.com

Library of Congress Cataloging-in-Publication Data

Names: Kurucan, Ahmet, 1961- author. | Altay, Korkut, translator.
Title: The ultimatum : does the Qur'an command killing non-Muslims? / Ahmet
    Kurucan ; translated by Korkut Altay.
Description: Clifton : Blue Dome Press, 2023. | Original Turkish title Baris Esastir. |
Includes bibliographical references and index.
Identifiers: LCCN 2023014443 (print) | LCCN 2023014444 (ebook) | ISBN
    9781682060346 (hardcover) | ISBN 9781682065419 (ebook)
Subjects: LCSH: Jihad. | Murder--Religious aspects--Islam. |
    Terrorism--Religious aspects--Islam.
Classification: LCC BP182 .K87813 2023 (print) | LCC BP182 (ebook) | DDC
    297.7/2--dc23/eng/20230508
LC record available at https://lccn.loc.gov/2023014443
LC ebook record available at https://lccn.loc.gov/2023014444
Printed in India

Contents

Preface VII

Preface

On April 21, 2018, the French daily *Le Parisien* published a manifesto demanding that "the verses of the Qur'an calling for murder and punishment of Jews, Christians, and nonbelievers be struck to obsolescence by religious authorities," so that "no believer can refer to a sacred text to commit a crime."[1] The manifesto was signed by some prominent figures, including former President Nicolas Sarkozy.

There are four Qur'anic verses that can be translated as, "Kill those who associate partners with God wherever you come upon them" (in chapters al-Baqarah, an-Nisa, and at-Tawbah). There is also a saying (*hadith*) of the Prophet, in which he is reported to have said, "I am commanded to fight people until they say, 'there is no deity but God.'" The manifesto is an indication of how much the Qur'an is misunderstood and the grave need for the clarification in the meaning of the scripture, especially in matters that relate to violence. In this book, I am trying to unearth the original meaning of these verses and the *hadith*.

As you will notice in the coming pages, I have primarily focused on the first-hand addressees of the revelation process: the Prophet's Companions in Mecca and Medina, and the polytheists of the time. What did they understand about these verses? How did they act in response? Considering these verses in relation to the conditions and events of the time, who were these verses addressing? Who were the polytheists these verses were referring to and what had they done?

---

1   Karina Piser. "Muslims Recoil at a French Proposal to Change the Quran," *The Atlantic*. May 3, 2018.

Today, trying to understand and interpret Islamic sources without proper knowledge of the historical context is a major problem. Muslims believe that the Qur'anic teachings appeal to all of humanity; they are not restricted to a certain era and place. However, many verses were revealed in the context of a real-life situation and regarding an immediate community. These verses can be correctly understood when they are considered together with the background conditions and factors. This is an essential step in the interpretation process of such verses, especially for us who did not live in that immediate community.

Detaching the verses from their actual context makes it impossible to reach the right meaning. Without the actual context and perspective, the text can be interpreted in a literal sense and be used to suit anyone's own wishes. Since examples of this mistake were already seen during the lifetime of the Prophet's Companions, first-generation scholars who compiled the essentials of Islamic teachings were very scrupulous about this issue. By building the principles of *usul al-din* (methodology of religion), they tried to prevent misinterpretation of Islamic teachings.

A correct understanding of the verses in question is of crucial importance.

Islam came as a Divine Mercy to humanity. Attributed to Fakhr al-Din al-Razi or Bayazid al-Bistami, the following definition is a comprehensive one: "Religion means paying due respect to God and showing compassion and mercy to the creation." We can infer from this definition that all commands and values brought by religion are meant to serve these two purposes.

If this is so, and given that polytheists are also a part of creation, is it right to kill them? Extending the question further, is there not an incompatibility between the verses meaning, "there is no coercion in religion," and "whoever wills (to believe), let him believe; and whoever wills (to disbelieve), let him disbelieve" and the verses about killing polytheists?

There have always been people trying to legitimize their terrorist activities by interpreting verses through superficial reference to scripture, as there still are today. Our discussion in this book will clearly reveal how baseless such references are.

Within this frame, I make occasional references to real life examples in order not to let our points remain too theoretical. One such example is the fifth verse of chapter Tawbah, known as the "verse of the sword," and how it is understood by the infamous terrorist organization, ISIS.

The Qur'an and the Prophet's traditions are available for all of us to explore. As for understanding and interpreting them in an insightful way, it is a difficult task of great responsibility—for this world and the next. This is what I have tried to do with this modest work now in your hands. I pray that my intentions are pure. Our duty is to work; then we expect guidance and support from God.

Acknowledgments

First of all, I would like to thank Enes Ergene, a fellow intellectual and a dear friend, who contributed to this book immensely. He worked on the manuscript line by line and shared with me his comments and revisions. Throughout our friendship of many decades, I have always benefited from his extensive scholarship. I also would like to thank Mr. Ömer Çetinkaya for his careful copyediting and useful comments. Also, heartfelt thanks to Dr. Hüseyin Şentürk from Blue Dome Press, who has offered encouragement, patience, and gentle care since the beginning of the publishing process. Finally, I would like to express my gratitude to my dear wife Zehra Kurucan for always bearing with me during my studies and long writing hours.

Ahmet Kurucan

JIHAD

1

JIHAD

Jihad ranks among the most debated concepts in Islamic political, legal, and intellectual history. Many underlying reasons for this pertain to historical, legal, theological, political, and ideological factors. The concept has a broad scope of reference—including "to combat," in the literal sense. Thus, it is not surprising to find substantial differences of opinion on how to understand certain Qur'anic verses on this matter.

The debate around "jihad" became even more heated in the second half of the nineteenth century with the rise of colonialism and invasion of Muslim lands. As a result, the concept became loaded with an unprecedented amount of political and ideological meaning.

We will elaborate on the etymological roots of the concept in addition to its definitions and forms of classification in the terminology later in the book. We need to note that this recent semantic overstretch—to a more political and ideological dimension—has led to new debates and intellectual endeavors among Muslim thinkers as they seek to explore new definitions with the help of other Qur'anic concepts. These studies have generally been centered on reconciling the interpretations of jihad in Islamic jurisprudence, theology, and intellectual tradition of the classical period with the modern paradigms.

Just as there are some political, religious, and civil structures that adopt violence and conflict as the center of their basic discourse in all nations, so do such groups within the capillaries of Islamic societies. The contemporary so-called jihadist Salafi currents exemplify such groups with their acts of violence and harsh behaviors. These "jihadist" interpretations have formed a conception of Islam with no regard for any hierarchical and systematic approach to Qur'anic verses and concepts and have thus broken away in thought and belief from the classical traditions of Islamic jurisprudence, theology, and politics. As a matter of fact, the reason they have been hanging on to the concept of jihad is because they see it as an argument for realizing this substantial breakaway.

This move is not only a jurisprudential or theological split, but one that is also philosophical and ideological. The "society" that such movements and interpretations aspire to form is only realizable with such a substantial epistemic breakaway from the tradition of mainstream Islamic thought.

It can be argued that only a few concepts, if any at all, can rival jihad in terms of their psychological influence and authority over Muslim peoples' conception of belief, ethics, society, politics, and ideal human. Jihad has a wide scope of definitions that include diverse fields. These include calling others to Islam (*dawah*), self-purification (*tazkiyah*), and range from creed (*aqidah*) to ethics (*akhlaq*), from family to the conception of society, and from politics to—in the broadest terms—civilization.

The concept of "*qital*/making war," for instance, is frequently mentioned in the Qur'an and has historically been a matter of extensive debate among Muslim jurists. However, *qital* has never had a spiritual and psychological influence as wide as the concept of jihad. Considering the limited scope of conditions, and the exclusivity of the concept of "*qital*/war," it is obvious that it is not as comprehensive as jihad and cannot contain the sweeping radical changes and transformation certain groups desire in Muslim societies.

Qital can provide the basis for political/ideological opposition and struggle against a foreign power colonizing and invading your land. People can be organized around the concept of *qital* to form a national resistance for freedom. But, if the goal is to generate a transformation *within* an Islamic society, including in ethics, religious doctrine, politics, and education, then the more convenient concept is "*jihad*."

From lecterns to public speeches, and from personal to societal preferences, jihad is an ever-handy argument and has always been the mantra and argument of all groups that adopted violence, conflict, dissension, and revolution. Since jihad is so conveniently available for the aforementioned purposes, it has not been possible to reach a systematic definition based on a conceptual, philosophical, and legal hierarchy.

Is the concept of "jihad" really a picklock which opens every door and solves all ethical or social problems? Does it justify every method and render legitimacy to every thesis? Is jihad a "tabula rasa" concept that, when loaded with provocation, can motivate Muslim masses in every direction?

Undoubtedly, the concept of "jihad" has a spiritual and psychological effect that determines, interprets, and manages all reflexes of Muslim societies. The entirety of the internal dynamics of communicating Islam is under jihad's influence and spiritual authority.

Historically, Islam has been a source of spiritual and moral transformation in every society that has adopted it. For this transformation to be maintained, developed, and regenerated anew in every generation, Islam has preached the concept of jihad to the faithful. What lies at the heart of Islamic revelation is the human being and its moral and spiritual transformation. This internal transformation is expected of every individual, and it is the actual womb where the concept of jihad is conceived. When the noble Prophet and his Companions were returning home from a battle, he told them that they were coming from the lesser jihad back to the greater jihad, pointing out that the real jihad is one's inner struggle for moral and spiritual transformation.

Over the centuries, the concept of jihad has expanded in meaning. The Qur'anic verses and the noble Prophet's statements already present this concept in a very broad perspective. However, different political, social, and international problems faced in the Islamic world over the last century have led to rather extremist constructions of meaning around jihad. In particular, the emergence of "jihadist" movements such as al-Qaeda, ISIS, the Taliban, and al-Shabab has caused a semantic "shrinking" of jihad: many now perceive it to be identical with war and violence. Today, the concept of jihad has turned into a paradigmatic problem that generates the most anxiety both within Islamic societies and in the West due to this narrowing of meaning. Many Islamic thinkers are making a tremendous effort to correct jihad's demonized image in the Western mind.

In the Islamic world, however, many civil and political organizations continue to abuse the concept. The power "jihad" brings to mobilize masses in the direction of their political and social aims has also brought a sort of immunity. Such groups dislike definitions that delineate the scope of jihad in Islamic law, theology, and politics, and they perceive it as a direct assault against Islam itself. The main concern of these radical groups is that they will lose the power they extract from "jihad" if their followers can form a consensus around jihad with common sense and moderation. There are entities and persons that are nurtured by the concept of conflict and war between different civilizations. It is obvious that such groups welcome a concept of "holy war," for this would support their thesis.

The fact that "jihad" has such a broad spectrum of influence in religious, ethical, political fields, and international relations makes it more difficult to write about it. Every attempt for a new definition brings in additional influence on the current considerations that are informed from it. No matter what the extent and nature of such effects will be, defining the concept on correct Islamic, literal, and ethical grounds is a task that falls to Muslim thinkers. Muslims are not the only reason why "jihad" is associated with a harsh and abominable meaning like "holy war" in the Western mind, yet the task of correcting this misconception is their responsibility.

Transformation of jihad into a political/ideological argument

Today, the concept of jihad has been encaged in an ideological frame of reference. Muslim societies that were subjected to colonialist invasions over the last few centuries have endeavored to give meaning to their movements of resistance. This construction of meaning, which was initially made with lawful causes and good intentions, effected a spirit of mobilization in Muslim societies, since theirs was a struggle for independence and liberty. Not all regions of the Islamic world experienced occupation, yet many Muslim nations have had to live under a long-term Western hegemony. Colonialism and occupation have a long history in those lands, which nurtured the mindset of "us vs. them."

Those who led the struggles to save their states and nations from Western hegemony drew on the motivating power of religion to activate masses and named their struggle as "jihad." They did have a point in this use of the term, and many politicians, generals, and religious scholars used it in this sense as well. In addition, there was evidence in Qur'anic verses and the Prophet's statements and practices that could be construed as foundations for their arguments.

On the other hand, as mentioned above, the word "jihad" has always had a very broad spectrum of meanings in Muslim societies. When Muslim lands are under attack and fighting back to defend the country is inevitable, jihad provides a more ethical, effective, and extensive frame of reference—especially considering the destructive and disastrous consequences of war, which not only threatens the political and military existence of a nation, but also have a huge impact on their religion, moral values, perceptions on the human and society, and all in their possession. Therefore, the concept of jihad provides an extensive psychological basis and support in such a context—much more than the term "*qital*/war" does. It is vitally important to understand the concept of jihad in its own framework; otherwise, it suffers a narrowing of meaning to be identified primarily with "*qital*/war."

Historically, Muslims have a long and extensive experience of war. As they expanded geographically, so did the scope of threat against their existence. Their encounters with the empires around them caused them to find themselves in a psychology of constant warfare. The long Middle Ages is a history of empires that were inclined to expand their borders and annex other lands by destroying other civilizations. Almost all of them were based on an ideal of conquering the world. For centuries, relations between different empires and civilizations were nearly limited to warfare and were defined in a dichotomy of war and peace. Nobody could meet any foreigner in their lands with the exception of visitors who came either as envoys for negotiations or for trade.

Not unlike the rest of the world, Muslims determined their political and military dynamics according to one of the two following statuses: war or peace. The concept of "holy war" was a slogan of Christian empires for many centuries, and it aimed at maintaining military unity against Muslims. The sole outward motive for this colossal mobilization call was religion.

In response to this, Islamic states clung to the concept of "jihad." In the backdrop of these centuries-long military struggles, jihad was emphasized more for militaristic purposes and at the expense of its personal, moral, ethical, and social dimensions.

The debate on jihad is not exclusive to the long Middle Ages. The colonialist period that followed and invasions of some Muslim lands in the twentieth century gave way to new political and ideological activities that called for mobilization once more around the concept of jihad. However, the resulting new formations were completely different from their historical counterparts. These were new experiences and organizations, without a precedent in the past, but with a new militia spirit. This was not an action adopted by any Muslim government. It rather manifested as a fundamentalist opposition within Islamic societies firstly directed against their own state's political and legal structure and practices, as well as the state's secularist worldview. Then, radical sectarian groups of varying sizes began to spring up with an exaggerated sense of self-importance, their worldviews as the center of everything, and themselves as saviors with a megalomanic spirit.

However, those formations were not able to generate a sufficient, substantial domestic discourse: the concept of jihad needed a real foreign threat or war; an ideological or legal opposition or difference of opinion would not serve the purpose. Therefore, these movements needed international crises to grow their ideologies and have a bigger societal impact. The ongoing crisis in Palestine, the 1979 invasion of Afghanistan by Russia, the Bosnian genocide, the 9/11 attacks, and other similar developments helped these narrow ideologies to gain a more influential position in Muslim societies. In this context, jihad has become the most essential argument of legitimacy for both legal Islamist political organizations and radical groups organized as militia forces.

The concept is so welcome to these groups that they use it not only to generate a thesis and tool of propaganda at an international level but also to summon masses within Muslim societies not pleased with the existing governments. While their essential domestic concept is based on a sectarian, moral, and partially political transformation, their message to the world involves claims of a new caliphate and Islamic union against imperialism, colonialism, and anything they perceive as a threat to religion.

Despite a long and diversified historical experience, jihad is still a very central concept, if an ambiguous one, for Muslim societies.

Jihad in essential texts

The previous section presented a general outlook about the concept of jihad and the background of its use in politics, the military, and religion as well as how it was conceptualized in the early, middle, and later periods of Islamic history. In this section, we will explore this concept as it is found in the essential texts of Islam and how it manifested in the practices of the Prophet, whose choices constituted the foundations of the religion.

There is an abundance of scholarly research and intellectual debate devoted to studying the essential texts of the classical period. Although these studies have proved to be very useful in many aspects, they have also caused much confusion in many people's minds. This is partly due to the failure of academic research to keep up with the constantly changing political and socio-cultural context that gives way to new developments and debates. Terrorism and violence are chronic realities. No matter the reasons, we are living with this reality, and we keep holding meetings and symposiums, and sign political treaties seeking solutions against the destructive consequences of terrorism and violence. This comes with a very high material and spiritual toll. It seems that as far as this volatility continues, studies too will continue to go adrift.

Let us remember here a few classifications of jihad as found in almost all of the classic texts. The first is the difference between "greater jihad" and "lesser jihad." This classification is based on a *hadith* report, albeit its authenticity with regards to the chain of narration is debated.[1] Accordingly, actively engaging with an enemy on the battleground is defined as "lesser jihad," whereas "greater jihad" is a person's inner struggle against the *nafs* (the carnal soul), which is defined in Islam as a person's greatest enemy.

Although the narration is a weak one from a scholarly aspect, it is possible to find other authenticated sayings of the Prophet to support this meaning. For example, "True *mujahid* (maker of jihad) is a person

---

1   Fakhr al-Din al-Razi, 23/72.

who starts jihad against his own soul."[2] Ibn Taymiyyah rejects this categorization, for he believes that the initial narration is not authenticated. According to Ibn Taymiyyah, fighting against unbelievers is one of the greatest deeds.[3]

Despite disapproval from scholars like Ibn Taymiyyah, this first classification has been widely accepted throughout history, for it finds its basis in certain narrations critically analyzed by scholars of *hadith* and Islamic mysticism.

The second classification defines jihad as human struggle in four areas: 1. Seeking knowledge; 2. Social engagement; 3. Military; and 4. Struggle against the carnal soul. Jihad in "seeking knowledge" means intensive intellectual endeavor. Jihad in "social engagement" is every action, measure, and effort aimed at public benefit by way of supporting the community, promoting solidarity, supporting the poor, encouraging good relations, and protecting people from any harm. "Military" jihad refers to taking a physical action as a final resort when keeping peace via diplomatic relations is no longer possible, such as when there is an enemy attack by another state or similar situation where brutal force is used. And finally, struggle against the "carnal soul" refers to a person's very special and systematic endeavor for self-improvement and spiritual/moral transformation to reach a desired state of purification. All of these four categories fall under the title "jihad."[4]

There is a third classification preferred by many scholars of different schools of Islam, including the great Hanafi scholar Kasani, which defines jihad as the struggle made with heart, tongue, hand, or sword.[5] Accordingly, believers struggle against the devil and carnal soul with

---

2   Tirmidhi, Jihad, 2.

3   Ibn Taymiyya, *Majmu ul-Fatawa*, 11/197.

4   For this and other classifications of jihad, see "Dinler ve Cihad" [Religions and Jihad] by Cafer Sadık Yaran, in *İslam Kaynaklarında, Geleneğinde ve Günümüzde Cihad* [Jihad in Islamic Sources, Tradition, and Today], Kuramer, Istanbul, 2017, p. 49-55.

5   Mustafa Öztürk, "Cihad Ayetleri: Tefsir Birikimine, İslam Geleneğine ve Günümüze Yansımaları" [Jihad Verses and Their Impact on Heritage of Exegesis, Islamic Tradition, and Today], in *İslam Kaynaklarında, Geleneğinde ve Günümüzde Cihad*, Kuramer, Istanbul, 2017 s. 49-55.

their "heart"; they encourage others to do good and forbid evil with their "tongue"; prevent existing evil with their "hand," and battle against the enemy with their "sword."

Let us mention right away that "preventing evil" is something that falls under state authority, and the state enforces this by means of security forces and law. Any act otherwise will mean vigilantism, with individuals seeking to claim rights of their own accord. Obviously, this will not bring order but chaos.

Let us now take a look how the military sense of jihad took their place in the Qur'an, in the light of the natural course of the Prophet's life. The life and practices of the noble Prophet—except perhaps those that pertain to his person as a human—were centered on communicating the Divine message. The Prophet's life and actions are accepted as essential, binding principles, and that is why they very meaningful and important for all Muslims. However, it requires scholarly endeavor to determine what these principles are and in what way they are binding on Muslims.

What is more binding than the Prophet's practice is God's will, and in the matter of jihad, some Qur'anic verses express the Divine will directly and in the form of an ultimatum with no reference whatsoever to the messengership of the Prophet. This emphasis and style of expression in such verses may be inferred to indicate the intervention of God's transcendent Willpower with history. In other words, God is acting, as it were, as direct agent in certain rulings without having the Prophet's messengership as a tool to convey to people—this may sound inappropriate in theological terms, for in religious literature the Prophets, the scripture, or the angel are all recognized—based on a Qur'anic decree (*nass*)—as intermediaries for the Divine Will and purpose of God Almighty. These types of revelations that represent the Divine Will exist in other holy scriptures, too. Such a discourse can be interpreted as God's direct dialectic with humanity and society. Many scholarly works produced throughout Islamic history can be seen as products of such a dialectic.

There have been some modernist views that have undermined the historical role and even the prophetic mission of the Prophet, too. However, such views have not been adopted by the larger Muslim society and remain marginal.

During the 23-year mission of the Prophet of Islam, the Qur'anic revelation came with direct reference to certain situations. This way, the verses resolved many religious and social problems within the context of those situations, which would shed light for later generations on how to understand these verses correctly. Many Qur'anic verses address specific occasions, like the battles of Badr,[6] Uhud,[7] and the Trench (Handaq),[8] treatment of war prisoners,[9] Peace Treaty of Hudaybiyah,[10] conquest of Mecca, campaigns of Tabuk and Muta, the way to observe prayers during warfare, and the like. There are tens, even hundreds, of issues emphasized in the historical and practical context. For example, a woman named Hawla bint Sa'laba argued with her husband Aws ibn al-Samit and then came to the Prophet to complain about this issue. The first four verses of the chapter al-Mujadilah were revealed in connection with this complaint and settled the disagreement between Hawla and her husband.

We can give other examples showing the direct relation between the Divine decree and the immediate society. In fact, the Qur'an directly refers to the situation of Zayd ibn Haritha's divorcing his wife, Zainab. Another chapter refers to Abu Lahab by name and by saying "his wife" also refers to Umm Jamil and demonstrates their antagonistic attitude. In brief, as seen from these examples, it is not possible to imagine the Qur'an as independent from the human being, human realities, and from societal life in the most general sense.

What matters is Muslims' conception of the meaning of verses and how they apply this meaning to real life. Surely, Muslims accept that the Qur'an has a super-historical quality as Divine address—namely, it gives general decrees and principles even when referring to a particular real-life example. Together with that, if we do not study the contextual aspect of Divine address effectively with the particular real-life situations they refer to, we will inevitably fail to develop a healthy and insightful commentary. When we take into consideration the schol-

---

6   Al Imran 3:123-127, Anfal 8:7-12; 42-44; 67; 71.

7   Al Imran 3:121-122; 14-144; 152-157; 165-171.

8   Al-Ahzab 33:9-25.

9   Al-Anfal 8:67-69; Muhammad 47:4.

10   Al-Fath 48:18-28.

arly heritage of the classic period, particularly classic texts of Qur'anic exegesis (*tafsir*) and legal methodology (*usul al-fiqh*), we can see a very efficient dialectical relationship established. We know that those classics do not adopt a general theological approach, which takes verses like metaphysical decrees abstracted from the historical context and which ignores their reasons for revelation and disregards their practical correspondence to the individual, society, and law.

Let me acknowledge once more: it goes without saying that the Divine Word has to be understood, discussed, and interpreted in accordance with the transcendent Divine truth. However—as it is also seen in the classics of Islamic scholarly heritage—principles of jurisprudence and final conclusions drawn from them need to be discussed in a very rationalist way with reference to the human, logical, legal, and political context. If the situation had been otherwise, no scholarly disciplines and commentaries in Islamic tradition would exist. But they do exist, and they approached and discussed the revelation within the corresponding context of the verses.

The disagreements and tensions about interpretation of verses and judgments sometimes led to serious intellectual, political and even international problems.

It is not a coincidence that this tension intensifies when it comes to the interpretation and practice of the verses about war and certain other verses fighting against the aggressor polytheists. Interpretation of those verses keeps being a cause of tension both in terms of traditional methodology and in terms of international paradigms and norms in modern times.

In the classic methodology of Qur'anic exegesis, there are two principles that relate to our topic here: A word should be construed as having some meaning, rather than passed over in silence; and, particularity of the causes of revelation (*asbab al-nuzul*) does not prevent drawing a general principle or judgment from it.

Accordingly, the meaning of certain verses that were revealed in response to a specific event has been applied to other general situations, keeping the scope as wide as possible. This was considered as a unique indicator of the superhistorical nature of the Qur'an. However, it is a fact that such substantiation has been applied to very few cases. In other words, historical and practical experiences indicate that these principles were not adopted in all matters.

This substantiation of Qur'anic verses' being superhistorical has been made within the framework of Islamic disciplines. That is, these disciplines have contributed to the process of substantiation with their own methodology and principles and built an extensive ground of thought. Despite this contribution, the matter is yet to be solved, and there is still no conclusive method of interpretation and systematic thinking that can be considered universally convincing and satisfactory, which is one of the underlying reasons why there are calls around the world to denounce certain Qur'anic verses, like the French manifesto mentioned in the Preface of this book.

One wonders how appropriate such calls are, for raising questions about the ontological truth of a holy scripture is usually an inefficient and mistaken path that leads to provocation. It is wrong to approach a sacred text—even if they are the ancient gnostic and Hermetic texts which are as old as 5,000 years—with such a tactless and provocative style. There are established systematic and methodological ways of interpreting both those texts and sacred scriptures. Interpreting a scripture from within its own exegetical tradition and applying it accordingly to new situations and to new social and historical developments should yield sounder results.

Even a colony of bacteria begins a struggle for survival when they perceive a threat to their existence. For religious people, revelation does not only stand for a form of belief and lifestyle; it determines the entire meaning of their existence. That is why calls like the French manifesto, which might raise ontological problems about a sacred text, are likely to provoke masses of believers. In this respect, both politicians and international strategists must act with the utmost self-possession and responsibility. Otherwise, they do not only make no contribution to a possible solution, but also become an obstacle against any optimist views about them. No outside call can have a real influence in the capillaries of a society.

A greater responsibility falls to today's Muslim thinkers. Besides, we are living in an age of communication. Every kind of data, including provocative and manipulative statements, spread quickly throughout the world. It is obvious that such international threats are among the prime sources that provide advantages to radical organizations. However, examples from within Islamic history demonstrate that the groups who favor a radical understanding of those verses do not really have strong intellectual and traditional references to support their discourse. On the contrary, even in the eras when Muslims were at the peak of their power, they did not interpret those verses like radical groups do today. It is possible to show hundreds of examples. Take, for instance, the following verse: "... kill them wherever you may come upon them..." (at-Tawbah 9:5). The plain truth about this verse is so obvious: had it been possible to interpret this verse by ignoring any context or principle of methodology, then Islamic history would have merely consisted of war and killing. At its face value, it is possible to say that this verse commands killing polytheists not only during warfare but even in times of peace. However, this has never been the case. Although the command to kill is mentioned in five places in the Qur'an, Muslims never started a wholesale state of war against the polytheists at any time in history. This indicates that the above-mentioned verse was taken together with other verses with the Qur'an within a definite method and system, and it was interpreted accordingly.

In addition, no scholar made a statement like, "given that killing those who don't believe is a Divine commandment in the Qur'an, then not killing them will make each Muslim who does not do so a sinner." Had they said so, then they would not be able to explain the verse meaning, "God does not forbid you, as regards those who do not make war against you on account of your Religion, nor drive you away from your homes, to be kindly to them, and act towards them with equity. God surely loves the scrupulously equitable" (al-Mumtahina 60:8). Obviously, this would be a serious contradiction. Not to mention the example of the Medina city-state after the advent of Islam, where Jews, Christians, and polytheists lived alongside Muslims in accordance with the treaty they made.

Taking this verse at its face value means that every Muslim should transform into a warrior who tries to kill polytheists and unbelievers everywhere they see them. History proves otherwise. Had it been the case, those happiest about it would probably be radical jihadist organizations that spawn here and there in the modern world. This would give them very strong and chauvinistic feelings, causing an upsurge in their

hatred, destruction, and violence. In reality, since they do not care much
about the methodology and limitations of the scholarly tradition of Islam, they somehow find this motivation with their own misinterpre-
tations. War and conflict in every situation are the sole resort of these
marginal groups who assert such interpretations.

It is a definite fact that the verse meaning "... kill them wherever you may come upon them ..." (at-Tawbah 9:5) and similar verses
have busied the minds of everyone thinking about this subject. When
those who detach the verses that pertain to war both from their relevant
context and the general purposes of the Qur'an saw the narrowness of
thought and interpretation they were doomed to, and they tried to develop different theories to justify their stances. The issue of abrogation
(*naskh*) is one of these subjects. Normally, abrogation is a tool for us to
see how the Divine communication occurred in close correspondence
with the first Muslims' social practices, life experiences, difficulties, and
their process of adaptation to Qur'anic principles. As a matter of fact, it
is possible to trace the same correspondence in many other verses that
did not undergo abrogation. Examples of this process are taught to exemplify an essential principle of interpretation in classic methodology
studies of Qur'anic exegesis and Islamic jurisprudence.

Certain groups have turned abrogation into an overcharged theory beyond its actual scope. With this theory, especially jihadist groups
think they eliminate the so-called outward contradiction between
Qur'anic verses; they raise the perception that they provide a legitimate
basis for their reactionary acts and discourses. As becomes obvious
when the entirety of the Qur'an is taken into consideration however,
they fail to see that their discourses and methods wreck the general
purposes of the Divine address and the public welfare it endorses. For
the sake of justifying their marginal group's interests and inclinations to
violence, they go as far as to disregard the injunctions of tens of other
verses. Probably the sharpest and clearest example of this mistaken approach is the fact that ISIS claims that the fifth verse of chapter at-Tawbah (*ayat al-sayf* - "verse of the sword") eliminates hundreds of other
verses which are in favor of peace. This is what they think and believe.
They probably do not even take the method of "abrogation" – which
they assert in this elimination – as a theory; they rather perceive this as
a clear Divine command to be followed with fervor of worship, because

jihadist organizations' general perception of the Qur'an does not follow any systematic thinking. Theirs is an extremely literalist understanding that puts all emphasis on the face value of words. No need to emphasize how shallow, dim, strict, and distant from wisdom and virtue this understanding is. They do not engage with history and take meaningful lessons from it. What they produce is nothing but a senseless human profile, nourished by war and violence, robotic creatures who have lost their consciences. During warfare, they take as basis the guerilla lifestyle, which they spend only by reading the Qur'an and mostly watching movies of fighting and war. In such a lifestyle, there is no place for wisdom and truthful philosophy. In the hands of such people, the Qur'an is simply a book carried along for taking oaths to die, to kill, and to destroy. In this respect, the verses about jihad and war are virtually like lifebuoys they hold onto.

Their theory of abrogation serves them as a way of justifying their actions, providing inner relief, and, most importantly, as a manifesto to organize their fight. However, this kind of literal and face value interpretations abstracted from other verses and the general purposes of the Qur'an (*maqasid*), their historical context, and their relation to other verses, leads to greater contradictions and bigger problems both for them and Muslims in general.

Note that even the theory of abrogation they cling to does not suffice to solve the contradictions and problems. This is why those who realized this insufficiency have tried to seek scholarly ways out with concepts such as conditionality (*takyid*), specification (*takhsis*), suspension (*ta'lik*), preference (*tarjih*), and purposes (*maqasid*). Interpreting Qur'anic verses requires a perspective that sees the injunctions in the verses as Divine intervention to history between the years of 610-632; it needs to take into consideration the context of revelation and give priority to the intended meaning. Throughout history, this perspective has been adopted by scholars who opposed the literalist mentality. Books of methodology are full of such scholarly work. Since these profound and rich methodologies and experiences are not drawn on sufficiently, the shallow and outward religiosity we call "hearsay Islam" becomes prevalent, which works to the advantage of the radical groups we mentioned.

There are also historicist approaches on this matter, especially in academic circles, which deal particularly with the verses that feature implications of violence in their external phrasing. Some of the thoughts we will express here might outwardly sound similar to these approaches. However, we are not disregarding or rejecting the classic heritage of thought by basing our views on a general assumption, as historicists do. Our approach in this book includes the principles and perspectives observed in the methodology of jurisprudence and in the tradition of Qur'anic exegesis, which were also observed by early-generation scholars in their understanding of the Prophet's life. In their works, we see the first mental efforts into how the Qur'an dealt with unfolding events along the process of revelation, including which verses came in relation to which happenings, what their meaning was, and how these meanings were put to practice.

Although these efforts did not draw on a properly systemized scholarly methodology in the early period, they are accepted as the first steps in understanding the Qur'an. Concerning that period, we can say the following at least: until the geographical and socio-cultural expansion via conquests took place, these first experiences would answer every religious question that arose in the early Muslims' social practices, without any need for the more complex interpretation methods and intellectual tools needed later on. There weren't many complicated and different cases in early Islamic society. There was no need for an arduous intellectual effort to tackle with any differentiation between new situations and the Qur'anic verses along with the words and practices of the Noble Prophet and of those who followed him. In other words, since the life conditions of the period of revelation changed very slowly in the early years of Islam after the Prophet, both Qur'anic verses and the example of the Prophet with regards to his words, actions, judgments, behaviors, and acceptances would suffice without need for new interpretations.

However, this was not the case for the later periods. With conquests and rapid expansion, Islamic society came into contact with foreign cultures and with new religious, administrative, and moral systems; Muslims could not keep their plain form and suffice with those early reflexes anymore—and they did not. The development and growth were happening so rapidly that the community of the period of revelation was being replaced by an entirely different and gigantic caliphate.

In comparison to the great and radical changes experienced during the Industrial Revolution and the following periods, the change experienced in Islamic society on account of the expansion is minor. Even contemporaries of the industrial revolution failed to envision the cultural and social upheavals it entailed. These upheavals gave birth to different sciences, like sociology and economics, and each of these disciplines tried to understand and interpret the colossal problems and changes caused by modern industrial society.

Very similarly, most of the Islamic disciplines were born during the period of *tadwin* (codification) in response to the extensive conquests in order to understand the socio-cultural transformations of society and to come up with scholarly answers to the emerging social situations. To some extent, Islamic thinkers had envisioned this substantial change. Especially in assumptive jurisprudence, they had already laid the foundations of a theoretical methodology to enable scholars to cope with possible questions and challenges. In other words, scholars of the era of codification did not discuss the problems they were confronted with merely in a jurisprudential form.

Likewise, other scholarly disciplines of Islam did the same thing in terms of their own field. Almost in unison, they tried to envision the reflexes of Islamic society before the new situations, and every branch of study came up with arguments to help rebuild society in their own field. The entirety of the scholarly studies made during the era of codification, which took place during the three centuries after the Prophet, is a clear indication of our point. The scholarly Islamic disciplines that were systematized in that era formed the methodological base for Muslim societies to cope with the religious, political, administrative, moral, and social problems they would encounter.

Even though those disciplines took an effective role at directing and shaping the reflexes of Muslim societies, it is not possible to say they always effectively and comprehensively dealt with every new situation. Actually, it is a historical reality that there were certain shortcomings at scholarly activities in a very early period. Namely as it happened with all long-term, unchanging traditions of thought, there were obstructions and problems in Islamic traditions of thought as well. In short, early period Islamic societies did not undergo the kind of rapid and radical changes seen in modern times. Hence, thanks to the intellectual traditions and methodologies systematized in the era of codification, they tried to cope with new situations and problems, and they generally succeeded.

Although problems got more complicated, and more complex forms of society emerged, those traditional solutions still coordinated Muslim societies' religious, moral, and socio-cultural reflexes for many centuries. In other words, time was still flowing quietly. In those times when change and transformation took years or even centuries—unlike ours—even the outward meaning of verses and the Prophet's sayings for the most part provided satisfactory answers to the problems faced. And in situations when this did not suffice, scholars would act and try to generate new solutions with their methodological interpretations and judgments.

In early Islamic society, two different attitudes emerged with regards to their stance before new situations: *Ahl al-Hadith* (Traditionists) and *Ahl ar-Ray* (Rationalists). Traditionists only took as basis the literal meaning of the commandments and from the perspective of their own understanding of religiosity; they saw it as more proper and safer to adopt a conservative attitude before new developments and situations. By acting with an understanding of solely text-based religiosity, traditionists became one school of thought, which, in the long run, has adopted a more reactionary mode in the face of new events.

Rationalists, however, developed around the city of Kufa where they practiced their scholarly and jurisprudential activities. From the earliest steps, this school maintained a correlation between religious teachings, social environment, and changes. It established its methodology to "read" these changes and develop appropriate commentaries. In time, it has influenced other schools of thought to adopt the principle of reason (*aql*) and independent reasoning (*ijtihad*)—which would be associated with the founders of the Hanafi school later on. This school of jurisprudence, where reasoning took a more effective role, developed further over time and formed the basis of both jurisprudential activities and some matters of belief.

Over time, the rationalists started to be represented by the Hanafi and Maliki schools in jurisprudence, and by Maturidis and Mu'tazilites in creed, who prioritized reason in their opinions. The traditionists were represented by Shafii and Hanbali schools, and Asharites. The former saw that the outward meaning and suggested meanings of the existing decrees would not suffice in the face of new developments and brought reasoning into more functional use. The latter acted in the opposite way and instead of developing new interpretations and giving scholarly responses, they focused on a possible solution restricted to the outward meanings and scope of the existing decrees.

Jihad verses, war, and peace

The Qur'anic verses on *qital*/war were revealed in reference to different historical events. Yet almost all of them relate to one and the same context: valid reason for war. "*Qital*" expresses a state of war when Muslims are in active battle with the enemy. It is a collective action declared by a legitimate state based on certain conditions (such as when the enemy does not incline to peace, initiates the attack, etc.). We need to see the distinction between being in direct engagement with the enemy and a person taking on this collective commandment as a personal initiative to "kill" in any given condition. Both cases are subject matters within the "law of war" of classic Islamic jurisprudence. Since the early days of Islamic legal formation, scholars and jurists made serious deliberation over these verses. They developed methodological thoughts on how these verses should be understood and the situations in which they refer to individual actions or fall within the law of war.

Jihad is derived from the root *j-h-d*, which is also the root for many other words like *yujahidu, tujahiduna, jahid, jahidu, jahd, juhd, mujahidun,* and *mujahidin.* It is important to follow a method in order to understand the verses that contain these words—many scholars of methodology have occupied themselves with this endeavor across many centuries. Given that the outward meaning of a verse is clear, our method here will be to revisit the context in which these verses were revealed. This requires considering the verses' order and reason of revelation. Every meaning drawn without knowing the circumstances, reasons for revelation, and time of revelation will cause a misunderstanding.

Given that there was Divine intervention with these verses, then we first have to understand what the Divine Will "says" in the text of the

Scripture. I want to underline the difference here between the "letter" and the "spirit" of the Scripture, for without knowing the letter first we cannot know the latter. The spirit of the Scripture can be deciphered with access to disciplines that provides us with the details of history and context (like *hadith*, history, *seerah*, and *maghazi*). Without referring to those disciplines, Qur'anic exegesis is not possible.

In order to understand verses correctly, it is not simply sufficient to know the reason and order of revelation. Most of the books of exegesis, particularly those based on narration (*tafsir al-riwayah*), report the events concerning the verses whose reason for revelation is known, but they do not give much background information. Perhaps, they assumed that people living in a certain place where similar conditions prevailed would already know the details and avoided too much elaboration; however, background information that clearly presents the social, political, cultural, and economic aspects—namely, knowledge of the context—is no less important than knowing the reason for revelation. Such a knowledge is helpful to understand what sort of circumstances the verse was revealed about and what possible solution it prescribed. In this respect, one can even say that it is compulsory to know the pre-Islamic Arab society. Pushing aside the pre-Islamic period on the basis that the Age of Ignorance brings no good, will mean sabotaging our own task. Demonizing the pre-Islamic era with sweeping comments for the sake of extolling Islam is not a proper approach. Qur'anic exegesis (*tafsir* and *ta'wil*) is not possible without the details provided by the disciplines that study history and context. Interpretations detached from the actual context might drift us out of the meaning intended in the Scripture.

Once we understand what verses *say*, then we come to what they *mean to say*, particularly to us, and how the verses address our time. Without doubt, the first source to be referred for that purpose is the practice of the noble Prophet and then interpretations and practices of Islamic scholars throughout history.

Secondly, we have to consider the process of tradition from the time of the Prophet's Companions up to our day: how this issue was understood and practiced, and which theories were developed around these meanings. When we place these two components in the center and then look into the concept of jihad, we see that scholars have made very different classifications, a few examples of which we mentioned above. In my opinion, to understand jihad in a military context, and thus within the "law of war," we first need to seek an answer to this question: What is essential in international relations according to Islam: peace or war?

The answer to this question relates as much to theories of international relations as it does to Islam. While the entirety of the terminology that relate to this issue—holy war, incessant warfare, defensive war, *dhimmi* (a non-Muslim minority living in Muslim land), *harbi* (a non-Muslim alien entering Muslim land), land of war (*dar al-harb*), land of Islam, land of peace, temporary truce, *jizya* tax, etc.—forms the building blocks of these theories on the one hand, they also enable us to reach a conclusion on the other. Even more importantly, these theories were formed around the doctrines built upon the practices of the noble Prophet and his Companions.

When the founding scholars of the early period formulated these theories, they gave priority to two concepts: war and peace. Naturally, everybody is but a child of their own time. After all, we are talking about theories, which were generated by people, based on the data at their disposal. To put it in the language of religious literature, they made "*ijtihad*" or scholarly deduction of new judgments. Those pioneering scholars, who were also children of their own time, were naturally under the influence of all existing and possible factors that could have any effect on society and the state, in the short or long term. For example, those who placed "war" in the center of international relations—Imam Shafii (d. 820) being the first—argued that non-Muslims formed a collective front against Muslims, and that they always sought war to exterminate them. Historically, when circumstances of warfare overlapped a backdrop where religious affiliation was the main component of social identity, some moved forward to specify that "disbelief" (*kufr*, namely not accepting the Islamic faith) was a valid reason for war.[11] When this state of constant warfare gained speed across wider territories, some jurists even took this idea further to argue that in order not to let Islamic

---

11   Abu Bakr Ahmad al-Bayhaqi, *Ahkamu'l-Qur'an li'l-Imam Shafii*, Beirut 1990, p. 389. Ahmet Yaman, *İslam Hukukunda Uluslararası İlişkiler* [International Relations in Islamic Law], Fecr publishing, Ankara 1998, p. 111-127.

armies lose their practical ability to fight, it was necessary to wage war every ten years against countries considered to be a land of war (*dar al-harb*)."[12]

I am not condemning any scholar for stating their ideas. When I said above, "Everybody is but a child of their own time" and referred to the prevalent circumstances as an important element, I tried to point out that those scholars reached their conclusions with certain rational foundations of their own. A different attitude would be anachronistic, which is neither a scholarly nor a fair approach.

A "war doctrine" formed within such background conditions and with subheadings like war, peace, and combat ability has to sit on a substantial theoretical basis. In such a case, the Qur'an is the first source to be referenced, for sure.

Now, let us take a look at how those who adopted war as essential to Islam classified the verses of jihad. The classification I will quote is from a paper by Talip Türcan, in which he takes a comprehensive look on the Prophet's life in Mecca and Medina (610-632). His commentary looks into the thesis that places warfare in the center of international relations with references to the reasons and timeline of revelation, and also traditional scholarship. A brief summary of his commentary and the evidence he offers are as follows:

1. Verses from the early Meccan period:

"There is no coercion in religion" (al-Baqarah 2:256);

"... do not care (whatever) those who associate partners with God (say and do)" (al-Hijr 15:94).

In these verses, we see an emphasis on freedom of belief. In that period when the balance of power was in favor of polytheists, it is com-

12   For first-hand sources of discussions conducted by scholars of different schools on this issue, see: Talip Türcan, "Fıkıhta Cihad" [Jihad in Jurispredence], in *İslam Kaynaklarında, Geleneğinde ve Günümüzde Cihad* [Jihad in Islamic Sources, Tradition, and Today], Kuramer, Istanbul, 2017 p. 288, footnote no: 30.

manded that Muslims communicate the Divine message without any coercion and without making even verbal struggles.

2. Verses from late Meccan period:

"Do not argue with those who were given the Book save in the best way, unless it be those of them who are given to wrongdoing (and therefore not accessible to courteous argument)" (al-Ankabut 29:46).

"Call to the way of your Lord with wisdom and fair exhortation, and argue with them in the best way possible" (an-Nahl 16:125).

Considering that the Meccan period lasted 13 years, it is commanded that they engage in conversation with polytheists and People of the Book, who were familiar with Islam by then to a certain extent. This remains so until the migration to Medina.

3. The period right after the migration to Medina:

The verses that allow war came during this segment of time. However, there are two conditions about it: The first is the fact that the people who oppressed Muslims in Mecca wanted to continue this oppression in Medina, too, and second, that Muslims would accept it if the latter preferred peace. The following verses refer to this issue:

"Fight in God's cause against those who fight against you..." (al-Baqarah 2:190)

"The believers against whom war is waged are given permission to fight in response, for they have been wronged." (al-Hajj 22:39)

"And if they incline to peace, incline to it also, and put your trust in God ..." (al-Anfal 8:61)

4. Declaration of war outside the sacred months:

"Then, when the (four) sacred months (of respite, during which fighting with those who associate partners with God and violate their treaties was prohibited to you,) are over, then (declare war on them and) kill them wherever you may come upon them, and seize them, and confine them, and lie in wait for them at every conceivable place. Yet if they repent and (mending their ways) establish the Prayer and pay the Purifying Alms, let them go their way. Surely God is All-Forgiving, All-Compassionate" (at-Tawbah 9:5).

This verse is known as the "verse of the sword." According to the opinion of those who accept warfare as essential, this verse marks the beginning of offensive – not defensive – war against not only those who are aggressors against Muslims but also those who are not.

5. The period when war was commanded in the absolute sense without the exception of the sacred months:

"(But if they persist in causing disorder, continue to) fight against them until *fitnah* (disorder, oppression) is no more, and the religion is recognized for God" (al-Baqarah 2:193).

Those who argue for ongoing warfare bring this verse as evidence. As a supportive argument, they also cite a saying of the Prophet in which he is reported to have said, "I am commanded to fight people until they say there is no deity but God."[13]

To sum it up, what we see here is a merely text-based reading which takes into consideration the order of revelation but not the reasons for revelation nor any knowledge of the context. Accordingly, the perspective of this classification brings us to no other conclusion, but that Muslims are supposed to be in unconditional warfare against unbelievers and polytheists constantly and ceaselessly. We need to remember that these interpretations were made under circumstances when non-Muslims were nearly in a state of total war against Muslims, which make these interpretations understandable.

---

13   Talip Türcan, "Fıkıhta Cihad" [Jihad in Jurisprudence], *İslam Kaynaklarında, Geleneğinde ve Günümüzde Cihad* [Jihad in Islamic Sources, Tradition, and Today], Kuramer, Istanbul, 2017 p. 281.

Before we carry on with the counter arguments of those who say, "peace is essential in Islam," let us point out one thing clearly: the state of peace or war is not a solely religious matter: in real world affairs, war or peace is not declared only for religious reasons. An approach otherwise goes against human nature and the natural course of life. This does not mean that there cannot be religious reasons for war or peace. History bears witness that religious reasons have played a role in war or peace.

> "God does not forbid you, as regards those who do not make war against you on account of your religion, nor drive you away from your homes, to be kindly to them..." (al-Mumtahana 60:8).

We can inversely deduce from this verse and from historical realities that during the revelation process, some fought against Muslims solely out of religious difference. What happened back then may happen again at present or in the future. However, a holistic look tells us that religious difference is not always the dominant factor and a main reason for war. Historically, political, economic, and other reasons have played a much greater role than religion as reasons for war. After all, we are talking about international relations and war as its final and undesired form, and these fall within the field of politics. Therefore, let me underline once more that although religious difference can be among the reasons for war, it must be acknowledged that war is essentially a political issue. In the context of the battles the Prophet had to participate, we see his state leadership ahead of his Prophethood. Islamic scholars in the past and present accept in unison that the Prophet's example and decisions prior to, during, and after any war, along with relevant Qur'anic verses, are binding upon Muslims. Then how do those who argue that peace is essential—including myself—comment about the verses of jihad?

Those who prioritize "peace" explain every verse by looking into several aspects of a given verse: the reasons for revelation, timing and order of revelation, and detailed knowledge of the context and background conditions. This is different than others who take the order of revelation as the sole basis and claim that only the verse "… fight against them until there is *fitnah* (disorder, oppression) is no more ..." (al-Baqarah 2:193) is essential and that all of the preceding verses are abrogated.

This difference of perspective constitutes the main reason for the two sharply contrasting conclusions about the issue.

For those who take warfare as essential, in the first phase of Islam (the early period in Mecca), the relentless pagan enemies were the dominant power while Muslims didn't have forces to respond with physical struggle and thus there were verses like, "There is no coercion in religion," (al-Baqarah 2:256) and "Do not care (whatever) those who associate partners with God (say and do)" (al-Hijr 15:94). While those who take warfare as basis argue "these verses are abrogated," those who take peace as basis state that these verses retain their validity in all times and places.

The perspective of those who favor peace takes as basis not the existence or absence of power to struggle against enemies. For them, freedom of religion and belief—or absence thereof—is what matters, for religion is an issue that needs to be chosen wholeheartedly and without compulsion. In other words, one of the most essential wisdoms and purposes of peace is protecting and maintaining freedom of religion and thought, for the "peace" emphasis of Qur'anic verses and Prophetic traditions does not merely relate to the issue of freedom of belief and thought but to the entirety of human life. Compulsion by interfering in a person's belief is prohibited by numerous verses. This prohibition is exemplified in the life of the noble Prophet as well.

In the second phase of Islam, according to those who prioritize peace as essential, verses emphasize peaceful and sensible ways: "Call to the way of your Lord with wisdom and fair exhortation..." (an-Nahl 16:125). This and other verses that enjoin peaceful ways (such as al-Ankabut 29:46) are not abrogated at all and have a superhistorical meaning.

The third phase began right after the migration to Medina and permission for war against the Meccan polytheists (the Quraysh tribe) and is marked by the following verse:

> The believers against whom war is waged are given permission to fight in response, for they have been wronged (subjected to *zulm*). (al-Hajj 22:39)

As is known, the Qur'an gave permission for war with this verse and brought "*zulm* (oppression, wronging, cruelty)" to the fore as the reason. Now the question that needs to be asked is: how do we elucidate "*zulm*" here?

We can find the answer to this question by looking into the Prophet's life, specifically in the Meccan period and the two-year Medina period until the Battle of Badr. After the permission for war in verse 39, simply reading the following verses answers what is meant by *zulm*:

> Those who have been driven from their homeland against all right, for no other reason than that they say, "Our Lord is God" (al-Hajj 22:40).

Here we see two things in terms of the definition, meaning, and nature of *zulm*. One is that the Muslims were obstructed from freely practicing their faith and the other is that they were so persecuted, they had to leave their homeland. They were not allowed to practice their faith freely in their homeland. According to those who say, "warfare is essential" in the 4th or 5th phase, the command of this verse was abrogated by the verse that commands a total state of war against polytheists and unbelievers:

> "(But if they persist in causing disorder, continue to) fight against them until *fitnah* (disorder, oppression) is no more, and the religion is recognized for God." (al-Baqarah 2:193)

Some may say that there is no need for abrogation in terms of content, because the previous verse (22:39) is already referring to the same thing. This answer feels satisfying to the heart and convincing to the mind. However, there are other verses in the same phase that command peace. For example:

> "And if they incline to peace, incline to it also, and put your trust in God ..." (al-Anfal 8:61)

If we ever accept that war is essential, then how can we comply in real life with the command of this verse that commands Muslims prefer peace if others incline to peace? Those who take war as "absolute" and treat it as the ultimate judgment either ignore the meaning stated by this verse or try to block its judgments with principles of methodology, like

abrogation (*nash*), specification (*takhsis*), conditionality (*takyid*), preference (*tarjih*), and exception (*istisna*). However, if the verse's reason
for revelation, timing, and context are considered altogether, it will be
seen that the command for peace is not restricted to limited segments
of history, to peculiar circumstances, or to the granting of freedom of
belief in a certain phase of warfare.

Warfare is not a primary condition in human life, nor has it been
in human history. Likewise, the Qur'an takes war as a secondary condition and aims to establish peace; the outward meaning of the verse
2:193 is referring to a historical and special context. Also, contrary to
the claims of those who assume warfare as essential, all calls for jihad in
the sense of war and combat in some Qur'anic verses were revealed for
very exceptional and special conditions. Had the Scripture really taken
war and conflict as foundational, then Muslims would strictly be busy
with nothing but war and fighting. In that case, every passing day without war would mean going against Divine command. Muslims would
be supposed to mobilize all of their forces and means until not a single
polytheist remained on earth. Similarly, if Muslims were to take this
statement of the Prophet, "I was commanded to fight until Islam becomes the only religion on earth," then they would have to fight not only
against countries but against each individual on earth. Such an assertion
can neither be compatible with the simplest level of common sense nor
with any human, social, or religious realities. Even if it can be necessary
to fight for the sake of freedom of faith in certain situations, continuity
of these freedoms can only be maintained by the functionality of the
verses that command peace; this is the emphasis of the opinions that
take peace as their basis.

It is claimed that the fourth phase was marked by the declaration
of an outwardly absolute, general, and continuous state of warfare and
this approach was defended with reference to the "verse of the sword"
(at-Tawbah 9:5).

As mentioned before those who say warfare is essential claim that
hundreds of verses with themes of peace, tolerance, coexistence, and the like
are all abrogated by one verse. Let's quote the verse here one more time:

> "Then, when the (four) sacred months are over, then (declare war
> on them and) kill them wherever you may come upon them, and

seize them, and confine them, and lie in wait for them at every conceivable place. Yet if they repent and (mending their ways) establish the Prayer and pay the Purifying Alms, let them go their way. Surely God is All-Forgiving, All-Compassionate." (at-Tawbah 9:5)

A literalist reading detached from the reason for revelation and the context, lacking coherence with the verses that come before and after, and the order of revelation ignored, might conclude that the verse gives an obvious command to attack; that, Muslims can start the war and are supposed to kill polytheists in a relentless and ruthless fashion in combat for this sake.

What is the opinion of those who take peace as essential? To be able to understand the Divine command correctly, firstly the verse needs to be taken collectively with the accompanying verses. As our discussion develops, we will evaluate verses as a whole. But for now, let us make a few evaluations that pertain to the conclusion. The part from the beginning of the chapter at-Tawbah to the end of verse 24 is a group of interrelated verses with a collective meaning. To see and understand this, it is sufficient to read through a translation of these 24 verses; you don't have to know Arabic or be a scholar of Qur'anic exegesis.

Secondly, these verses are revealed in the form of an ultimatum against the Qurayshi polytheists who breached the treaty they had with the Prophet in his capacity as the head of state. These verses, as it were, put forward a declaration of war, which mark the termination of the treaty. Islam requires loyalty to agreements as part of ethical conduct and Muslims must comply with them until they are terminated. In this case, despite the fact that polytheists terminated the treaty by breaching its conditions, the Qur'an does not approve of a surprise attack in response. A similar tradition existed in the pre-Islamic era that gave the enemy a four-month period before the actual war. According to the same tradition of the Arabs, this declaration needed to be done by the leader of the tribe or one of his family members. When the revelation of these verses occurred, the Prophet was in Medina, and Abu Bakr was leading a group of Muslims to Mecca for pilgrimage. The noble Prophet sent his cousin Ali ibn Abi Talib after them to Mecca to declare this "ultimatum" (*bara'ah*) which is another name of this chapter and the reason why it does not start with Basmalah ("in the name of God, the

All-Merciful, the All-Compassionate"), the only exception out of all 114 chapters which do.

The second verse of this chapter allows polytheists four more months to live freely in these territories, which is also a period of respite before the actual war. While the treaty has been terminated, a declaration of war is also issued. Similar principles of warfare law have found their places in various international treaties from nineteenth century onward, with their sanctions determined.[14] This demonstrates that humanity was able to adopt the Qur'anic teaching of respite before declaring war only after many centuries.

Let us ask: can such a verse ever be taken to mean, "war is essential in Islam"? How is it possible to interpret it to command ceaseless warfare?

Thirdly, it is clearly understood from the verses that succeeded 9:5, the polytheists loyal to the treaty are out of the scope of this declaration of war. This indicates that the Qur'an does not accept warfare as an absolute principle; even when a practical situation that necessitates war arises, Islam brings ethical limitations to warfare and excludes those who remain loyal to any treaty signed between them. Also, had war been the sole and ever-valid principle, then it would be impossible for a country of Muslims to ever make any peace agreements with a non-Muslim country. Even the first Islamic state presided over by the noble Prophet signed many treaties, a fact which verse 4 of chapter at-Tawbah clearly expresses:

> Excepting those among the people who associate partners with God
> with whom you made a treaty, and who have not thereafter failed
> to fulfill their obligations towards you (required by the treaty), nor
> have backed anyone against you. Observe, then, your treaty with
> them until the end of the term (that you agreed with them). Surely
> God loves the God-revering, pious (who keep their duties to Him).

Fourthly, the statement in the verse "... kill them wherever you may come upon them, and seize them, and confine them, and lie in wait for them at every conceivable place," is about those who refuse to

---

14   M. Yasin Aslan, "Savaş Hukukunun Temel Prensipleri" (Essential Principles of Warfare Law), *TBB Journal*, Issue 79, 2008, p. 237.

make peace, who breach peace agreements time and again, and who are on the battlefield armed to kill Muslims. Namely, this commandment is for situations when parties are in war and it is not possible to maintain peace in spite of trying every diplomatic measure. How else can one behave when the fight has begun, and the other party is there to kill?

As clearly stated in the verses (at-Tawbah) 12 and 13, the polytheists were the ones who attacked Muslims first and broke their pledges. Therefore, "killing polytheists" is not an absolute statement to be adopted at all times; it refers to the Meccan polytheists of the time, and only applies to exclusive conditions. The exclusivity of this issue has been considered so significant that the names of those tribes referred to in this verse are mentioned one by one in relevant books of *seerah*, *maghazi*, and *tafsir*.

Fifthly, the same methodology used for the verses above can be used for other Qur'anic verses in relation to "killing polytheists." With that methodology, it will be seen that the Qur'an does not mention war as the only course of action against unbelievers. Each verse comes up with possible solutions that apply to specific situations with the conditions found in that verse's reason for revelation (*asbab al-nuzul*). Any commentary that ignores the specific circumstances that relate to that reason will lead us to misguided interpretations.

The final example we will give is the verse that is assumed as the basis for the claim that warfare against polytheists is essential (the fifth phase): "Fight against them until *fitnah* (disorder, oppression) is no more, and the religion is recognized for God" (al-Baqarah 2:193). As was the case for the "verse of the sword," those who take peace as foundational follow the correct methodology and, instead of detaching this verse from others, they interpret 2:193 together with the set of verses it happens to be among. Only then is it possible to correctly understand and interpret those statements that refer to the same situation. Otherwise, picking a single verse, or even picking half a sentence or a few words from the flow of the text, will never bring us to the correct conclusion. They bring to the fore, for instance, terms like "*fitnah*" with a disregard for methodology and for different frames of meaning along the course of history.

After having expounded on the verses that pertain to jihad, as well as the political theory around peace and war, we will focus more specifically on the Qur'anic verses about killing polytheists in the next section.

"Wherever You Come Upon Them"

Al-Baqarah 2:190-195

2

"WHEREVER YOU COME UPON THEM"

Al-Baqarah 2:190-195

As explained in the previous section, interpreting the meaning of any given verse has to be done in the light of the set of verses with which it was revealed. Taking verse 2:191 ("Kill them wherever you come upon them") in isolation to develop a political theory or mode of behavior based on that verse alone is wrong. We need to understand first what the verse meant in the historical context when it was revealed. For that to be possible, we need to consider the six verses, from 190 to 195, which relate to the same situation. Let us take a look at the context of verses: In the sixth year of the Hijrah (Muslims' migration to Medina), Hudaybiyah peace treaty was signed between Muslims and the Quraysh of Mecca. According to this treaty, a year after the signing of the treaty, the Qurayshi polytheists would abandon Mecca to allow Muslims to observe pilgrimage (*umrah*) for three days. When the time of this pilgrimage drew near, some Muslims were worried about the fact that previously, the Meccan polytheists had disregarded the tradition of not making war during the sacred months and that they might act in the same way again. The six verses we will discuss here were revealed under these circumstances.[1] Especially verse 194 states that respecting the sacred months must be observed by both sides, and that if the Quraysh

---

1   See *Kuran Yolu* [The Qur'an's Path], 1/270 and elsewhere; Ali Bulaç, *Kur'ân Dersleri* [Qur'an Lessons], Çıra Yayınları, Istanbul, 2016, p. 17414 and elsewhere.

breached the rule of not attacking, Muslims could respond in the same way. Now let us consider this set of verses in order.

Al-Baqarah 2:190

> Fight in God's cause (in order to exalt His Name) against those who fight against you, but do not exceed the bounds (set by God: do not kill children, women, and the elderly), for surely God loves not those who exceed the bounds. (al-Baqarah 2:190)

When the verse is considered together with its reason for revelation, it refers to a highly probable situation; and if this situation really arises, the verse describes the attitude to be taken by Muslims in response very clearly leaving no doubt.

The verse specifies that the permission to fight is "... against those who fight against you." This statement evidently shows that it is referring to a situation when diplomatic solutions have come to a dead end and Muslims are on the verge of an actual war.

Surely, Muslims have to fight back in a war that has practically started. In Islamic law, there are five essentials (*maqasid* or *al-daruri-yyat al-khamsa*): religion, life, property, mind, and family. Fighting to protect these is a person's right. These are acknowledged as lawful rights by other world religions and legal systems, too. "Fight in God's cause against those who fight against you" alludes to this right. However, this is immediately followed by, "but do not exceed the bounds, for surely God loves not those who exceed the bounds" (al-Baqarah 2:190), drawing red lines Muslims should not cross while engaging in this defensive fight. Although making such a defense is a lawful right, Muslims are cautioned against not committing any injustices or unlawful acts while defending themselves. It is a human reality that when people struggle to claim their lawful rights, they only focus on their own rights, and, in many instances, they are inclined to exceed bounds, particularly when they are under the psychology of victimhood and bear a grudge against their oppressors. The verse refers to this human weakness and demands Muslims to curb their vengeful feelings and heedfully observe rights and justice. This demand virtually has the nature and tone of a command. These verses were revealed in a context that necessitated laws of war, and Muslims are reminded to comply with them.

"Fight in God's cause"

The phrase "Fight in God's cause" is worth a separate discussion. This phrase is a good example of the theocentric language found in many verses of the Qur'an. The Qur'an is the holy scripture of Islam, a religion which stipulates particular and universal injunctions, principles, and rules based on certain events, and the authority of its scripture will continue until the end of time. In accordance with this belief, it is quite normal that the language of the Qur'an is different than secular language used in political, economic, and legal texts or other doctrinal documents. Phrases like "God's cause" brings to the mind of all Muslims implications of "lofty or high purposes." One may quote the Prophet giving references to this lofty cause. He was once asked when fighting becomes for God's cause, because some fight out of their anger, some fight for their pride. The Prophet said, "He who fights so that the word of God is made superior, then he fights in God's cause."[2] Such religious motivations have historically compelled many scholars to argue that Muslims cannot declare wars for reasons like occupying territories, spoils, dominating others, or gaining political influence. The reasons for this argument become clearer in the following five verses.

Religious texts in general emphasize the most ideal values and principles for humanity. The language of these texts, thus, comes in a binding theological form that reveals such lofty ideals. The most essential mission of Prophets is to put these ideals into practice in the most reasonable, understandable, and applicable way while taking into consideration human and societal realities. This is, as it were, the legacy of all God's messengers.

One important dimension of Prophet Muhammad's (pbuh) *sunnah* (his actions, words, and approvals) is that it represents the social and practical aspects of Islamic reason. However, human experiences do not always live up to these ideals. Islamic history has many episodes when Muslims' performances failed to overlap with these ideals. In in-

---

2   Bukhari, Ilm, 45; Jihad, 15; Ibn Maja, Jihad, 13.

terpreting Qur'anic verses on war and peace, Muslims' behavior has
shown many deviations from an ideal political perspective. Starting
from the selection of a leader after the death of the Prophet, early examples include the incidents like Siffin, Jamal, Karbala, and Mihna. The
fact that human behavior deviates from the ideals expressed by clear
religious injunctions (*nass*) legitimizes new analyses of the language of
religious texts. In other words, this widening between injunction and
action is the reason why there are different approaches to these texts.
The theocentric language of the scriptures is meant to encourage ideal
behavior and serves as an essential lexical source to maintain these ide-
alistic boundaries.

This does not make the holy scriptures detached from human and
social realities nor are its ideals beyond human nature and power. On
the contrary, these lofty ideals came in the form of a language system
which was a product of collective human communication, and this indicates the direct dialectical contact of holy scriptures with human experience. The fact that holy scriptures point to lofty ideas and purposes
more transcendently than could be possible with a secular language can
be inferred in relation to the human condition of being tested in this
life. While it is not always possible to reach the topmost purpose, set-
ting the bar this high is a precaution against a human's possible fall to
poor ethical conduct and mental depravity. For, Islam holds the human
as a unique being who is expected to make the best of the high ethical,
rational, and humane qualities they are blessed with. The high goals set
for every human are meant to prepare the person and motivate them to
work harder.

Going back to the relevant verse, we can also argue that Islam
sets certain ethical principles in the context of war and to bring human
weaknesses under control.

Al-Baqarah 2:191

Polytheism per se is not the cause of war

The second verse we will explore is 191 of chapter al-Baqarah. I am
going to give two alternative translations for this verse. The first will be
independent from the revelation's general concept and context, while
the second translation will be a paraphrased version by taking into con-

sideration all six verses as a set, along with the reason for their revelation. Here is the meaning of the literal wording:

> Kill them wherever you come upon them. And drive them out from where they drove you out. *Fitnah* (disorder, oppression) is worse than killing. Do not fight against them in the vicinities of the Sacred Mosque unless they fight against you there; but if they fight against you (there), you also fight them. Such is the recompense of the unbelievers.

Here is an interpreted translation in relation to the overall meaning of the text, context, and the actual message it gives:

> (O believers!) When you meet those polytheists on the battle-ground, kill them. You drive them out of Mecca, from where they had driven you out. The oppression, cruelty, exile, and torture they committed against you is worse than killing people during war. Do not fight against them in the vicinities of the Sacred Mosque unless they fight against you there; but if they fight against you (there), you also fight them. Thus is the punishment for the unbelievers who adopt a wicked attitude.

If you take the literal meaning as basis and read it by detaching it from everything else, you may conclude that "a continual and ceaseless warfare against polytheists is essential and they must be killed wherever they are caught," which is explicitly stated by those who claim, "war is essential."

According to this notion, unbelief by itself is the reason for continual warfare. However, such an assumption contradicts the conditional statement at the end of the verse where believers are allowed to fight back only when the enemy side starts the fight. Namely, the verse renders war conditional with such terms and thus there is no absolute continuity.

To reiterate, this set of verses came in relation to the possibility that the polytheists would breach the Hudaybiyah treaty and start war during the inviolable months when warfare is forbidden. The Hudaybiyah treaty, which was apparently not in favor of Muslims, was signed when Muslims wanted to visit the Ka'ba in Mecca for pilgrimage but were not allowed into the city by the Quraysh. According to this treaty,

Muslims could come back to observe their pilgrimage a year later. These verses are teaching Muslims the course of action to be taken if they are attacked, in violation of the treaty, when they return a year later during the sacred months. The Muslims of that time, who were the first people the Qur'anic message was initially addressing, understood the meaning of this set of verses according to this context of revelation. The translation of these verses, thus, must be done in accordance with the way they understood it. Otherwise, literal readings detached from the actual context might lead to misunderstandings, by attributing words to God He does not say. Therefore, the second extended interpretation of the verse (not the literal translation) better reflects the meaning.

The statement "Drive them from where they had driven you out," makes explicit who is being referenced. Who forced Muslims out of their town and homes? The polytheists of Mecca. Who covered hundreds of miles from Mecca to Medina to attack the Muslims at Badr, Uhud, and Handaq battles? Again, the polytheists of Mecca. So, the identity of the enemy was very explicit (note that the Meccans were not neutral non-Muslims; they had a long record of relentlessly attacking the Muslims and committing atrocities.

The Muslims of the time, the first community this verse was speaking to, already knew this. And the phrase "drive them out" in the verse refers to the polytheists who betrayed the treaty, as we have already established. The verse counsels a responsive act; but the first violation must come from the enemy. Otherwise, the verse would be commanding the Muslims to breach their treaty for no reason; such a conclusion cannot be drawn from this verse in any rational or textual sense. By mentioning "them" in the verse in reference to the polytheists of Mecca, the verse is actually exposing their attitude as the reason, as it were, for the consequences they had to face.

Does the verse refer to Meccan polytheists exclusively? If we are trying to understand the original meaning of the verse and asking what it is saying to those addressed in the first place, then, yes, it refers to the polytheists of Mecca. However, if you ask about the message this verse is giving to future generations of Muslims, it refers to people who adopt the attitude and behaviors of the Meccan polytheists.

According to the literal translation, the second sentence of the verse reads: "*Fitnah* (disorder, oppression) is worse than killing…"

Fitnah is translated in many translations as "persecution" (Pickthall), "tumult or oppression" (Yusuf Ali), "oppression" (M. Asad), and "disorder (rooted in rebellion against God and recognizing no laws)" (Ali Ünal). The word *fitnah* is usually used in the context of torturing people to force them to renounce their faith, persecution and oppression, establishing an order that denies God and associates partners with Him, violating basic human rights and freedoms, causing chaos and warfare with the tools maintained by disbelief and polytheism, tumult, or oppression.

In some languages, *fitnah* is used to connote "acting in a way to disturb peace in societal life and destroy unity," "badmouthing others," or "committing hypocritical acts"; but these are not used in Qur'anic translations. The word *"fitnah"* occurs in the Qur'an 34 times, and its derivatives also occur 26 times. With regards to their contextual meaning, they are used to mean "tribulation, pressure, torment and torture, calamity, misfortune, misguiding, insanity, suffering, sin, warring, and disorder." Note that there is nothing like "unbelief and associating partners with God" among the meanings of *fitnah*. Together with these, spreading unbelief and profanity, forcing people to give up their faith, acting in sinful ways, upsetting law and order, and driving people out of their homeland, is each a *fitnah*.

Considering the culture in Islamic lands, as people understand the word *fitnah* as an ordinary word in their language, they think they already understand it and do not give any consideration to the actual scholarly meaning here. Failure to note this fine difference naturally gives way to wrong interpretations and conclusions about the meaning of the verse. Therefore, while paraphrasing *"fitnah* is worse than killing,"* I would like to use the following wording which I believe reflects the meaning of the scripture better: "(know that) the persecution, oppression, exile, and torture they committed against you on account of your belief is worse than killing people at war." In line with this, for some scholars of Qur'anic exegesis, preventing *fitnah* is to prevent any danger of forcing believers to give up their religion, eliminating the risk of enemy attack, and maintaining freedom of religion and belief for everybody.

The verse ends, *"Do not fight against them in the vicinities of the Sacred Mosque unless they fight against you there; but if they fight against you (there), you also fight them. Such is the recompense of the unbelievers"* (al-Baqarah 2:191). In the pre-Islamic Arabian society, polytheists regarded the lunar months of Muharram, Rajab, Dhu al-Qaada, and Dhu al-Hijja as sacred, and it was forbidden to make war during these months. Even if a man met the murderer of, say, his father, he wouldn't do anything that would harm the murderer in observance of these months. Some said this practice existed since Prophet Adam, and some said it dated back to Prophet Abraham. In any case, the practice was upheld by the pre-Islamic Arabian society. The Qur'an requires Muslims to observe this ban during those sacred months, as stated in at-Tawbah verse 36:

> The number of the months, in God's sight, is twelve, as determined and decreed by God on the day when He created the heavens and the earth (and set them moving in the present conditions). Four of them are sacred (in that fighting is forbidden during them). This is the upright, ever-true Religion (the order that God has established for the operation of the universe and life of humanity). Do not, therefore, wrong yourselves with respect to these (four) months.

Note that here as well, it is said that it is not wrong to make war in response to the polytheists' offensive: "Nevertheless, fight all together against those who associate partners with God just as they fight against you all together; and know well that God is with the God-revering, pious who keep their duties to Him."

Al-Baqarah 2:192

Setting limits to warfare

The third verse I would like to focus on is verse 192 of chapter al-Baqarah. Here as well, I will give two different translations so that you can see the significant difference in meaning in comparison to a literal reading. The first one will be detached from context; the second will have context and paraphrase the verse's meaning when taking this into account.

The literal translation:

> "Then if they desist from fighting (you also desist), surely God is All-Forgiving, All-Compassionate."

The paraphrased translation:

"If they (polytheists of Mecca) give up attacking you, you do not attack them either. Surely God is All-Forgiving, All-Compassionate."

The second is of course a more accurate translation. Remember that this set of six verses was revealed when the Muslims on the way to pilgrimage were anxious of a possible attack by the polytheists. If you detach it from its context, then one may speculate as if warfare is not conditional, but that it is always essential in international relations; and that you can stop this constant warfare only if the polytheists cease fighting or give up, which would be a misinterpretation of the scripture.

On the other hand, even if we take the verse detached from its context of revelation and give the first meaning, there is no mention of ceaseless warfare in the absolute sense. The meaning of giving up attacks means decisively ending enmity within the frame of a permanent or temporary peace agreement, putting aside oppression and offenses, and living with mutual trust in an atmosphere of peace maintained by the treaty. As a matter of fact, we can see all of these examples in the life of the noble Prophet. As head of state, he did not turn down any people who asked for peace and who wished to remain in a neutral or non-offensive position, be it on the battleground or during normal times. He forgave everyone who asked for mercy. He did not show any enmity whatsoever against those who remained loyal to their treaty. On the other hand, the Prophet did not say no to fighting when legitimate reasons for war emerged, for instance when Muslims were attacked, the other party breached a treaty, when it was necessary to take counter actions against treacherous moves, or when they needed to defend against those who threaten faith, reason, property, life, and family (*al-daruriyyat al-khamsa*).

Strangely, the opinion arguing that "war is essential" centers around the verse we are going to discuss in the next section and asserts a doctrine of absolute war, but they do not consider at all the other verse in the same set of verses which commands Muslims to make peace. Sayyid Qutb even added disbelief as a condition and thus opened a door for making the comment that disbelief by itself is a cause of war. It is possible to see this approach in older works of exegesis as well.

Al-Baqarah 2:193

Freedom of religion

The fourth verse I would like to focus on is verse 193 of chapter al-Baqarah:

> "Fight them until this *fitnah* is eliminated and religion is exclusively for God. If they give up denial and violation, then know that there is no enmity against anyone but oppressors."

The original meaning of the word *fitnah* is exposing unprocessed gold to fire in order to distill it from foreign elements. As we explained before, in the terminology of Islamic scholarship, *fitnah* means committing persecution, torture, oppression, violating essential human rights and liberties, causing disorder and incitement, and the like. "Until religion is exclusively for God" complements this meaning. It is obvious that the words following this verse also complement the same statement: "If the polytheists give up their pressures, you do not attack them either." To put it more clearly, had it been possible to understand this in the sense that "it is lawful to make war with everybody until there is only Islam in the world and everybody becomes Muslim," then there would be a gross inconsistency in meaning. Namely, then this commandment would on the one hand require Muslims to comply with the conditions of the treaty and not to breach it unless the polytheists breached it; but on the other hand, it would require them to make war solely against others who believe in a different religion; this would obviously be self-contradictory.

Taking into consideration the reason for revelation, context, and coherence of the text, we can paraphrase the verse as follows: "Until the persecution and viciousness (by Meccan polytheists) is eliminated and religion is thoroughly for God—namely, there remains no one who persecutes people because of their belief—and until people are free to not have to answer to anybody because of their faith but to God alone, make war against the vicious polytheists who persecute you. If they give up their aggression and persecution, you do not make any attempts to attack them either."

This simply means if all individuals in society have freedom of religion and faith, then you do not have to initiate a war against anybody. As we see, "until religion is for God" does not mean until all non-Muslims in the world accept Islam; on the contrary, it means until people gain the freedom of accounting for their faith only before God. Such a meaning seems much more suitable not only for pointing out freedom of choosing religion and faith but also for understanding the verse in a way that befits the context in which it was revealed. Otherwise, it would weirdly imply that it would be lawful if Muslims resorted to brutal force to push all non-Muslims in the world to accept Islam, which is in complete contradiction with the essential peaceful principles of Islam.

The end statement that summarizes the main idea of the verse (*fazlaka*) is also very important: "... there is no hostility except to the wrongdoers." The specification by the last word here is very significant: "*zalimun*," which can be translated as "wrongdoers," "oppressors," or "those who commit cruelty."

It was perfectly possible to say the "polytheists/unbelievers" instead; and then those who claim that unbelief and polytheism in themselves are reasons for war would be right in their literal commentary. However, although the wrongdoers in question were polytheists and non-Muslims at the same time, they are not referred to as such; rather, they're referred to by their attitude of oppression. This is very clear evidence that disbelief, or in other words their religious identity, is not a reason for making war against them in an absolutist sense.

Can there be any historical factors underlying the attitude and interpretation of those who regarded disbelief on its own as a sufficient reason for declaring war? In my opinion, yes, there are. For example, the overwhelming majority of those who committed various atrocities against Muslims and continually fought them throughout the long Middle Ages were non-Muslims. The fact that Muslim states and societies were constantly at war, and that the aggressors were mostly non-Muslims, left a lasting impression in Muslims' memory. This effect inevitably made its way into the commentaries of religious scholars. However, a philosophical and intellectual look into them today will reveal that they were political, not religious, attitudes. Almost everything in previous eras was considered under the scope of religion and theology, which made it impossible to determine whether an attitude was motivated by religious, political, ethical, or philosophical reasons. Therefore, "disbelief is a reason for war" made better sense in their world.

The situation in the Christendom was not very different in the Middle Ages. Religion, politics, and philosophy were intermingled in their world as well. Perceiving these fields separately emerged only in modern times after the separation of science and religious disciplines. Today, we are able to distinguish concepts of political science from solely theological ones. However, there was no need for this distinction in the classical world. In short, every opinion expressed in those times had to be based on a religious reference. There were sufficient socio-political grounds for seeing disbelief as a reason for war. In reality, the actual problem was likely about perceiving political situations as solely religious.

Let me hasten to add that my intention is not to make sharp secular distinctions between what is religious and non-religious; this is not the issue here. Surely, every religion can have certain principles that can be considered political and even ideological. The point we are trying to emphasize here is that, when judgments that find a place in real-life politics are taken as purely religious ones, then it becomes more difficult to question them and to abandon them. Let us not forget that when religious motives are unified with human acts, they almost become inseparable. This is understandable to a certain extent, but there is the obligation to act objectively when making scholarly judgments. When religious reasoning and judgments of that period are viewed, the effects of the political atmosphere of the era can be seen.

Al-Baqarah 2:194

> A sacred month is retributive for another sacred month, and the inviolate values demand retaliation. So, whoever attacks you, attack them in like manner as they attacked you. Nevertheless, fear God and remain within the bounds of piety and righteousness, and know that God is with the God-revering, pious.

The point conveyed in the last four verses is repeated one more time in this verse in a way that puts a barrier before all misunderstandings and extremist interpretations. Therefore, we see no need to make additional comments. It is very clear that the verse decrees conditions to be observed during a warfare.

Al-Baqarah 2:195

"Spend" and "in the Way of God"

The sixth verse is al-Baqarah 195, and here is a translation:

> "(War or other defensive measures to maintain your existence, are not possible without expense, so) spend in God's cause (out of whatever you have). And do not ruin yourselves by your own hands (by refraining from spending. Whatever you do,) do it in the best way, in the awareness that God sees it. Surely God loves those who are devoted to doing good, aware that God is seeing them."

This seems to be the clearest translation which takes the context into consideration. The verse is not referring to a regular donation; it teaches Muslims how it is possible to raise finances when they need to engage a war, a war that is necessitated by legitimate reasons and which should be realized with justice. It even states that thriftiness in this regard can give way to great troubles in terms of protecting religion, reason, property, life, and family (*al-daruriyyat*)—that it may have ramifications even on future generations and that there is the risk of returning to earlier stages of persecution and torment. Naturally, not making the necessary financial preparations will result in defeat. Also note the theocentric tone in the phrase, "Spend in God's cause," similar to the one in "Fight in God's cause," explained earlier in this book.

At this point, I would like to give an example of how a verse can be misunderstood when the original context is ignored. During an attempt to conquer Constantinople, when a Muslim soldier was fighting rather recklessly without carefully protecting himself on the battleground, a Sahabi (a companion of the Prophet) warned him by quoting al-Baqarah 195: "Do not ruin yourselves by your own hands." From a military perspective, it can be said that it was a sensible warning supported with a reference from the Qur'an. But the meaning of this verse was detached from its context of revelation. The Prophet's famous companion Abu Ayyub al-Ansari corrected the other companion. He told him this verse was revealed at a time when Islam and Muslims started gaining power in Medina, and they were in a mood to settle down to deal with their worldly affairs as opposed to continuing to strive for Islam. So, the actual risk of ruining themselves was immersing themselves in worldly business.[3]

The second key word in the second sentence of the verse is "*ihsan.*" *Ihsan* means perfect goodness, doing good to others, acting God-consciously with the awareness of being in His omnipresent supervision, being well aware that everybody will be called to account before God for their actions, and thus adopting virtuous qualities. *Ihsan* and other words derived from the same root occur in more than 70 verses of the Qur'an. Its meanings can pertain to both God and human behaviors. By considering the richness of meaning in "*ihsan,*" the verse both commands acting in a God-conscious way and to follow a balanced and just attitude both during warfare and peace. We tried to give the translation to reflect both senses.

In short, *infaq* (spending/donation) and *ihsan* (perfect goodness) are Qur'anic concepts that urge Muslims to be considerate and responsible not only during wartime but in all of their intentions and actions throughout their lives. They need to be defined and understood within religion's universal framework of purposes that pertain to all aspects of life. Taking them in a sense that calls for a continuous warfare is a deviation of meaning.

To conclude, Islam does not command a ceaseless state of warfare as essential in international relations nor does it consider unbelief and polytheism on their own as sufficient reasons for war. To develop such a political theory or war doctrine based on Qur'anic verses 2:190-195, one has to disregard the context of revelation, textual coherence, and has to believe that these verses abrogate all previous verses that counsel peace.

Offensive or defensive war

The following question confuses many: the verses that command fighting brought a solution to the existing problems in relation to political

---

3   Tirmidhi, *Tafsirul Qur'an*, 3; Abu Dawud, Jihad, 22.

events at the time of revelation. We cannot say those verses were completely abrogated, but is it possible to say that war is absolutely restricted to defense?

We have already indicated in the previous section that warfare is not the basis of international relations based on the Qur'anic verses 2:190-195. Yet, we need to expound further on how Islam is a religion of peace. "Islam is a religion of war" and "Islam is a religion of peace" are both mere slogans and using them as such is wrong. I believe that such reductionist and cliché discourses are far from the methodology of the discipline and are an obstacle to sound understanding. War or peace is a political issue that pertains to international relationships. Those who will make such decisions are political authorities according to the circumstances of their time. Giving priority to peace is an ideal policy for sure. However, war is also a reality depending on conditions. A balanced pro-peace policy that does not ignore the reality of war as a human condition—and treats it as an undesired but a possible solution—better expresses the Islamic position.

War is a human reality, as history bears witness to. It has often been the final resort for those seeking salvation from injustice and oppression or when under attack. Although it has mostly destructive consequences, it often plays an inevitable role when other solution alternatives have been exhausted. If we are to develop a slogan for Islam, it is possible to say that Islam is a religion which prescribes "justice" as the basis of social relations; "moderation and integrity" as the basis of religious feelings; and "compassion and mercy" as the basis of human interaction with the whole of creation. For this is what Islam is: a religion of justice that commands compassion and mercy on all of God's creations: women and men, living and non-living, Muslim and non-Muslim, Arab or non-Arab, and any and all ethnic or religious identities.

The Ultimatum

At-Tawbah 9:1-24

3

At-Tawbah 9:1-24

I n chapter at-Tawbah (Repentance), there are verses with similar meanings to the ones discussed in the previous sections. A translation of the fifth verse of this chapter is as follows:

> When the sacred months (the 4-month term given before declaring war) are over, then kill the polytheists wherever you may come upon them, and seize them, and confine them, and lie in wait for them at every conceivable place. (at-Tawbah 9:5).

Just as we stated while expounding on the first set of verses (al-Baqarah 2:190-195), a literal reading that detaches a specific verse from the set of verses it is a part of, and that tries to extract new meanings but ignores the methodological principles (*usul*) like coherence within and across texts, the context, reason of revelation (*asbab al-nuzul*), and integrity of the Qur'an as a whole, results in a fragmentary and cursory reading. This is no different than, as it were, making God say anything one likes, and claiming, "this is God's will!" This, however, is the very approach of some marginal groups and those who wish to present Islam as a religion of violence. The message of God can only be understood by applying the methodological principles mentioned above. And this is what I will try to do for the verse at-Tawbah 5.

Except for the final two verses, the chapter at-Tawbah (al-Ba-ra'ah is another name for this chapter) was revealed in Medina. Various scholars of the classical tradition—like Fakhr al-Din al-Razi, al-Qurtu-bi, Ibn Kathir, Suyuti—commented that this chapter is a continuation of the previous chapter titled al-Anfal (the Spoils of War), and according to some of these scholars, this is why at-Tawbah is the only chapter that does not start with the name of God, the All-Merciful, the All-Compassionate (*basmalah*). Al-Anfal covers different subjects independent from one another, including judgments about war, God's help in lawful and just war, and distribution of war spoils. Considering this content in light of the contents of at-Tawbah, the aforementioned scholarly commentary makes sense. However, the first verse, "This is an ultimatum from God and His Messenger to those who associate partners with whom you have made a treaty...." is open to different commentaries.

Why this chapter does not begin with reference to God's compassion and mercy is perhaps better explained with the fact that this verse is an ultimatum (*bara'ah*), declaring in very clear terms, to parties who breached the treaty covertly or overtly, that the treaty is over and that diplomatic relations have ceased.

Let us now take a look at some of the reports that explain the circumstances of the revelation of this chapter: according to the information related by various sources, in the ninth year of the migration to Medina (*hijrah*) following the Tabuk campaign, the noble Prophet sent a group of 300 people to pilgrimage under the leadership of his loyal Companion Abu Bakr. The first 24 verses (or the first 28, according to some reports) of at-Tawbah were revealed after the group departed from Medina. Below, we will try to interpret this set of 24 verses as a whole by applying the relevant principles such as textual coherence and knowledge of the context.

In the first year after the conquest of Mecca, polytheists and Muslims were going to observe the pilgrimage (*hajj*) simultaneously. Muslims would not follow the pagan practices such as being stark naked during the circumambulation of the Ka'ba and not eating anything in the vicinity of this sacred landmark, but they would observe certain pilgrimage rituals side by side. For example, they would descend from Arafat to Muzdalifah together, as mentioned in verse 199 of al-Baqarah:

> Then (do not choose to remain in Muzdalifah without climbing
> 'Arafat in order to refrain from mixing with other people because
> of vanity. Instead,) press on in multitude from where all the (other)

people press on, and implore God's forgiveness (for your opposing Him in any way before now, and for the mistakes you have made during the Pilgrimage). Surely God is All-Forgiving, All-Compassionate (especially towards His believing servants)."

According to some reports, one of the reasons why the noble Prophet did not observe pilgrimage that year was the fact that the polytheists would be stark naked while circumambulating the Ka'ba.[1]

The Arab customs of the time normally required the Prophet himself or someone from his family to convey to the polytheists such a declaration as serious as the warnings in the first 24 verses. It was a declaration of war against polytheists who were not loyal to their treaty, with a four-month term of respite. In compliance with the custom, the Prophet assigned his cousin Ali to convey the verses and thus make the declaration. Ali ibn Abi Talib went to Mecca, and insistently emphasized the following four points in his address in the field of Aqaba: "Unbelievers will not find eternal salvation and will not be able to enter Paradise. After this year, no polytheist will be able to observe pilgrimage anymore and nobody will observe the circumambulation in the nude."

Those who still had a valid treaty with the Prophet could live according to the conditions of their treaty until the end of its term. However, those who breached the treaty or had no treaty at all were given a four-month respite after which they had to choose Islam or leave Mecca. If they demanded protection from Muslims in order to travel to a safe destination, their demand would be fulfilled.[2] Below, we will try to expound on each of these 24 verses.

---

1   See: İzzet Derveze, *et-Tefsirü'l-Hadis*, Düşün Yayıncılık, Istanbul 2014, p. 7/306. Originally published as Izzat Darwaza, *at-Tafsir al-Hadith*, Damascus, 1961-1963.

2   Bukhari, Tafsir, 1; Muslim, Hajj, 435. The fact that the Prophet sent Ali as his representative has been interpreted by the Shiites as evidence that Ali should have succeeded the Prophet as the legitimate head of state after the Prophet. This is not surprising given the fact the Shia reserves the leadership of the Muslim ummah exclusively to the family of the Prophet. However, this is an overstretched interpretation of what normally was nothing more than the local diplomatic custom.

At-Tawbah 9:1

This is an ultimatum

> "This is an ultimatum from God and His Messenger to those who
> associate partners with God with whom you have made a treaty."

It is clear that the addressee in this verse is polytheists; but which
polytheists? Most translations do not make the explanatory addition of
"those who breached the treaty." Although the first translation is outwardly correct, the real question here is which polytheists are being
mentioned, because the Qur'an refers to a certain group of polytheists here. Not including this additional but explanatory fact to translations can cause a reader to fail to understand the real meaning of the
Scripture. Actually, those mentioned in the verse are the polytheists of
Mecca—and particularly those among them who breached their treaty
overtly or covertly. Nevertheless, in the fourth verse, it will be obviously
seen that those who remained loyal to the treaty conditions are excepted
from this warning.

As a general principle, Muslims are bound by Islam to be loyal
to their treaties. Breaching a treaty with no valid reason means breaking one's word, which can never be compatible with the teachings of
Islam in any way. On the other hand, if the other side who signed the
treaty does not comply with the treaty conditions and breaches them
in an overt or covert fashion, then Muslims are not supposed to keep
complying with the treaty as if nothing has happened, as this can have
several ramifications against them. Therefore, if it is established via clear
and verified information from trusted sources that the other side has
breached the treaty conditions, then Muslims can also abandon their
compliance by regarding the treaty as invalid. This is a simple fact that
holds true for all treaties anyway.

However, there is an important detail here: When such a situation
did occur, it is conditional that Muslims declare to the other side that
they will not comply with the treaty anymore. This is clearly stated in
al-Anfal 58:

> If you have strong reason to fear treachery from a people (with
> whom you have a treaty), return it to them (i.e., publicly declare to

them, before embarking on any action against them, that you have dissolved the treaty) so that both parties should be informed of its termination. Surely God does not love the treacherous.

The verse above did refer to such a treacherous situation indeed. The polytheists of Mecca were convinced that Romans would rout the Muslims on the Tabuk campaign, and thus they breached the treaty by beginning to conspire against the Muslims while they were yet preparing for the Tabuk campaign.

Another point in relation to this verse is that God's name is also mentioned in the warning that the treaty has ended. This is in line with the theocentric style of the language used in the Qur'an and other holy scriptures. A fine line needs to be highlighted here: God is of course on the side of treaties that ensure justice, societal peace, and security for all—this is what He conveys to people via books and messengers, and what He expects from them. Otherwise, He is not in the paper of the treaty as a signatory like an individual. It should perhaps be assumed where God's consent lies in this situation.

On the wisdom of why the treaty was ended in this way, Izzat Darwaza comments that since some believers would have difficulty in understanding the wise purpose behind this and could hesitate at making a prior warning to polytheists as stated in the continuing verses, God's name is mentioned along with that of His Messenger. Thus, that probable hesitancy in Muslims is eliminated.[3]

One more point also needs to be underlined: that the Prophet entered into treaties of a political, economic, military, or any other "worldly" nature in his capacity as the head of state and on behalf of the nation he represented, not in terms of his religious duty as God's messenger.

At-Tawbah 9:2

The ultimatum put into action

(O you polytheists who always break the treaties you have entered into!) You may go about freely in the land for four months. But

---

3   İzzet Derveze, *et-Tefsirü'l-Hadis*, Düşün Yayıncılık, Istanbul 2014, 7/303.

know that you can never escape (the Power of God, nor frustrate
His will), and that God will bring disgrace upon the unbelievers
(sooner or later).

The latest developments caused the breaking of relations with the
polytheists of Mecca. If the Muslims had declared that relations had
ceased and demanding the polytheists leave Mecca *without* giving them
any respite would provide them with an excuse to argue that they were
wronged. Therefore, the four-month respite must be understood correctly: it gave them an opportunity to determine a new destination and
make the necessary preparations. The situation in question was not a
leisurely travel; a term of four months was long enough to find a new
place of settlement. Namely, there was no injustice made. Accordingly,
their continued presence in the vicinity of the Ka'ba and Mecca would
mean declaring war against the Muslims. This is referred by, "But know
that you can never escape (the power of God, nor frustrate His will)."
The verse is as if addressing the polytheists as follows: "Along a respite
of four months, the attitude you will take and your political and moral
position will be under surveillance. If you return to observing the treaty
conditions and stay in conformity of the socio-cultural structure of the
society, this attitude of yours will be taken into consideration. Otherwise,
you have no right to live here anymore." This is the meaning we infer.

Below is how the late scholar of exegesis Hamdi Yazır commented
on the meaning of this verse:

> "O polytheists who made a treaty (with Muslims) and to whom this
> address reached. Do not think that you will be wronged on account
> of a sudden invalidation of your treaty. You have a respite of four
> months from now on.
>
> Within this term, you are free to make any preparations you wish,
> free from worries of being assaulted. Since our diplomatic relations will
> have been completely ceased and warfare will begin, consider the safe-
> ty of your lives and property well. Take any kind of sensible measure.
> With regards to making preparations for war, preparing for defense, or
> finding a destination of refuge, you are given freedom to prepare well
> as you wish, within Muslim lands or other parts of the world."[4]

---

4   Yazır, Elmalılı Hamdi, *Hak Dini Kur'an Dili*, 4/267.

Another point to be made about this verse is answering the question, "which four months?" Does the stated term refer to the four months after the invalidation of the treaty or the sacred months during which Arabs forbade making war? Although some scholars said it was the four sacred months, there is no evidence that supports this opinion. According to the general acceptance of scholars, the stated term began on the 10th day of the month of Dhu al-Hijjah and ended after four months on the 10th day of the month of Rabi al-Akhir.

Let us reiterate the fact that the stated respite is for polytheist Arabs who breached their treaty. Considering those who do comply with their treaty or who do not take a hostile attitude against Muslims even if they have no treaty will not be considered within this scope.

At-Tawbah 9:3

> And a proclamation from God and His Messenger to all people on this day of the Major Pilgrimage: that God disavows those who associate partners with Him (and break their treaty), and His Messenger likewise (disavows them). (O polytheists!) But if you repent and give up hostilities, this will surely be for your good; but if you reject this opportunity and turn away again, know that you will never be able to escape God and frustrate His will in any way. Give glad tidings (O Messenger) of a painful punishment to those who insist on unbelief.

As it has no direct relation to our discussion, I will not go into the subject of major pilgrimage (*hajj*) and minor pilgrimage (*umrah*). Let me only point out one fact here: in contrast to the minor pilgrimage, there is a huge crowd on the days of Muzdalifah, Mina, and Jamarat (the symbolic stoning of Satan) when all pilgrims come together for the major pilgrimage. As we mentioned before, Ali ibn Abi Talib declared these first verses of chapter Tawbah and the four points emphasized with these verses to people on the first day of the Eid al-Adha, when the symbolic stoning of Satan happens. This is the year when by that time the polytheists had already left Mecca, i.e., the Ka'ba and the sacred territory in its vicinity in the aftermath of the conquest of the city. There was no pilgrimage in the old pagan ways anymore. In other words, it was the time when only monotheistic worship would be observed at the

Ka'ba, which was cleared of the pagan idols and what they represented. "God disavows those who associate partners with Him (and break their treaty), and His Messenger likewise (disavows them)" in the verse refers to this fact. The repentance (*tawbah*) mentioned in the continuity of the verse is meant in the sense of a demand that the polytheists abandon their long-standing hostile attitude against Muslims, that they should not conspire against them anymore, and not breach their treaty; thus, the "repentance" here is not the general sense of entreating God for forgiveness of sins. This is affirmed by "you will never be able to escape God and frustrate His will in any way" and the end statement (*fazlaka*) in the verse "Give glad tidings (O Messenger) of a painful punishment to those who insist on unbelief." The clear message here is a declaration that no additional term will be given after the end of the four-month term and warfare will begin afterwards. The *fazlaka* also reminds that what they will face in the hereafter will be much more severe than what may fall upon them in this world.

Muslims had suffered at the hands of the polytheists for many years preceding this declaration. As the polytheists lost their power after they lost Mecca to Muslims, this warning was a further consolidation of their retreat. Even in this situation, however, the polytheists were given an opportunity to repent for what they had done, to return or to leave Muslims alone and continue their lives elsewhere; this fact is important in terms of showing the practical dimension of Islamic principles of compassion, love, and justice. Note that it was the polytheists who breached the treaty, and there was no force around to prevent the Muslims from avenging themselves. In such circumstances, giving polytheists respite of four months to let them think about what to do next is an act of respect to essential human rights.

At-Tawbah 9:4

Polytheists excluded from the ultimatum

> Excepting those among the people who associate partners with God
> with whom you made a treaty, and who have not thereafter failed
> to fulfill their obligations towards you (required by the treaty), nor
> have backed anyone against you. Observe, then, your treaty with

them until the end of the term (that you agreed with them). Surely God loves the God-revering, pious (who keep their duties to Him).

We already know that all of the verses included in the ultimatum address the polytheists of Mecca; are all of them addressed here? No. The first verse of the chapter already states this meaning: "This is an ultimatum from God and His Messenger to those who associate partners with God with whom you have made a treaty but who breached it."

Those required to leave Mecca after a respite of four months were the polytheists who breached their treaty with the Muslims. In a commanding tone, namely in the form of a political ultimatum, the verse commanded Muslims to end relations with them. Therefore, this ultimatum obviously does not address the polytheists who kept their neutral position against the Muslims and did not engage in overt or covert cooperation with Muslims' enemies.

Excepting those who did not breach their treaty is significant. It encourages loyalty to agreements, which is an issue of separate importance from both political and ethical perspectives. Many other verses emphasize this ethical rule in different contexts. In addition, the noble Prophet made serious encouragements in this respect and often led by personal example. We see that once he gave his word, he would remain loyal to it against all odds. We understand that loyalty to one's word is a principle of utmost importance. The noble Prophet also mentioned "not being loyal to one's word" among the attributes of hypocrisy, which is another point of consideration. The subject matter of the verses we are discussing here is not a personal matter or something in between two people; it is in the field of politics and law. It is a reality that sometimes people go back on their word when they believe it is in the interest of their government in spite of agreements. It is important to note that scripture does not allow such conduct in international relations.

At this point, a question might come to our minds: "is it really humane to offer only three options to Meccan polytheists?" Does it not mean forcing them to choose between very limited options of joining the Muslims, leaving Mecca, or having to fight?

It does look so at first sight, but this ultimatum is not a judgment given as a result of events that took place in a few days. It had been a period of 22 years during which the polytheists were tested time and again during the mission of the Prophet; their attitude and behaviors were monitored in detail, and were a subject of many verses and decrees across all possible fronts: politics, belief, ethical, social, and human. A 22-year social experiment lies behind this conclusive ultimatum which came at a time when it was obvious that the polytheists were in no way open to living in peaceful coexistence with the Muslims. In this respect, even in the form of an ultimatum, giving three options and a respite of four months should be fair.

Furthermore, during the 13 years of the Mecca period, Muslims embraced a new faith and conveyed its teachings to others with gentle words and a mild attitude. In response to that, the polytheists constantly oppressed the Muslims. They committed torture, fabricated baseless rumors, accused Muslims of treachery, provoked their relatives against them, and exercised a prolonged communal pressure against believers. The Muslims were forced to leave their homes and emigrate to Medina. Even this did not satisfy the polytheists, and they went on to provoke everyone they could against the Muslims. They usurped all properties the Muslims left behind in Mecca and harassed their families. In short, the polytheists resorted to every kind of atrocity during the Mecca period.

Then came the Medina period. It is a long distance from Mecca and Medina (about 300 miles), and given the conditions of the time it was not an easy journey. Despite this difficulty, the polytheists of Mecca came all that distance only to assault Muslims in Medina. And they did not for once – over the nine years that followed the migration, they launched three major battles against the Muslims in addition to instigating many incidents of atrocity and provocation. They kept provoking neighboring tribes against Muslims. After they received a blow in their assault at the Battle of Badr, they grew even more resentful and made further vengeful plans.

Although they were dizzy with the partial success at the Battle of Uhud, their feelings of rage and vengeance did not abate. Their obstinate offensive resulted in the Battle of the Trench. Their alliance with other Arab tribes was not enough to soothe their national pride. So, they contacted other groups with different religious traditions, like some Jewish tribes, and sought different ways to increase pressure on the Muslims. They breached their treaty multiple times. We will suffice with this much, although it is possible to make a longer list of their atrocities. This 22-year period revealed the oppressive and unruly character of the polytheists who willingly destroyed with their own hands all material, social, and cultural means of coexistence. Given all this track record of crimes by the polytheists of Mecca, common sense requires us to see the options imposed by these verses to be nothing but low key, humanly options, even in terms of a modern understanding of international relations.

Another dimension to consider in this event was the fact that Muslims had a religious obligation to clear the Ka'ba of pagan idols. The options given to the polytheists were already providing this result, without need for war. Based on this event, many jurists rule that Muslims should accept when polytheists demand for peace and sign a new treaty with them, even if polytheists have breached their past treaties many times and declared war against Muslims—as long as the new treaty is in favor of the Muslims' interests. This approval can also be supported on the basis of the sixth verse in which God commands the Prophet to grant asylum to those who seek it and convey them to a place of security.[5]

In the *fazlaka* of the verse, it is stated that, "God loves the God-revering, pious (those who have *taqwa*)." Mentioning the concept of *taqwa* (which can be translated as God-reverence and thus acting virtuously) gives an essential principle and guideline for Muslims that they should follow an ethical conduct. Let us reiterate verse 5: "Surely God loves the God-revering (who act in compliance with their treaty in all of their behaviors, who keep their duties to God, who refrain from disobeying His commandments, and are scrupulous at not transgressing the limits He set)."

Giving translation of verses with their extensive meaning (sometimes in brackets)—in other words, awareness of inter-textual cross references, coherence of the text, reference to the actual context, reasons for revelation, and the holistic meaning of Qur'anic teaching—is important for gaining insight into verses. This is the very reason why we take verse groups collectively. Otherwise, an offhanded approach of tak-

---

5   İzzet Derveze, *et-Tefsirü'l-Hadis*, Düşün Yayıncılık, Istanbul 2014, 7/297.

ing verses in a detached fashion is doomed to distorted interpretations, like those made by extremist groups like ISIS and al-Qaeda.

At-Tawbah 9:5
The "verse of the sword"

> When the respite of four months—during which attacking them was forbidden—is over, then declare war against the offensive polytheist Meccans who did not keep loyal to their treaty and kill them wherever you find them, catch them and confine them. Do not let them act freely; surround them and prevent their escape by taking control of every conceivable place. However, if they repent, surrender to Islam and observe due responsibilities, open their ways and leave them alone. Undoubtedly, God is oft-forgiving of sins, and has abundant mercy and compassion for His servants who turn to Him repentantly.

Although the phrase "the sacred months (*al-ashur al-hurum*)" seems to imply the four-month ban on war as traditionally observed from pre-Islamic times, it makes much more sense to consider it in a wider scope and as referring to a universal principle.

In the time of Jahiliyya (pre-Islamic times), there was a well-established rule that banned fighting in four months: Dhu al-Qadah, Dhu al-Hijjah, Muharram, and Rajab. Islam adopted certain institutions and practices inherited from Jahiliyya. This was so not only because they were deeply entrenched in the society, but also because they were based on certain humane and ethical principles. Ban on war in these four months was one such custom. By adopting such customs, Islam is recognizing their value as a common heritage of human experience in the development of justice and fairness. There is even a principle in the legislative and methodological literature, called "*shar'u man qablana*" ("the [good] way before us") that establishes the legal grounds to adopt and continue this heritage from nations before Islam. However, it does not seem correct to restrict "the sacred months (*al-ashur al-hurum*)" in this verse to the traditional four months from the Jahiliyya. This four-month process is already a manifestation of the priority given to establishing an atmosphere of peace. Therefore, such a purpose cannot be realized by restricting this period only to certain months of the year. This also would not fit with a diplomacy of peace. For this reason, in my opinion this stated respite is to be taken as applicable to "the four months following the ultimatum." Though some early scholars interpreted this as the sacred months known in the pre-Islamic period, this was because of a literal understanding of the original term in the fifth verse *"al-ashur al-hurum,"* meaning "the sacred months," a phrase used in the Qur'an with reference to those months.[6]

As we have been trying to explain from the beginning, the verses in question are about the relentless attitude of the polytheists of Mecca who left the Muslims with no other alternative but war. Consequently, the verse explains the attitude and principles the Muslims should adopt about warfare.

The decision to make war is the final resort when all other solutions have been exhausted. We have to note here the fact that war is a state of mind that pushes back all mental and practical actions based on good will, while legitimizing and spurring on antagonistic feelings like rage, hatred, and revenge. War is destructive in all its aspects. It brings to the fore the animalistic side of humans: dying and killing, the euphoria of victory or the trauma of defeat—all of these turn battlefields into something inhuman. Nevertheless, sometimes war becomes an inevitable reality. So, Islamic teaching establishes ethical and humane restrictions to be observed during warfare. Especially in ancient times, war was another name for absolute lawlessness. Rules like not harming non-combatants (i.e., the elderly, children, and women) or not disrupting basic sources of human needs did not exist before Islam. Such principles found their way into the literature of law and diplomacy only in the late 19th century.

In addition to the points we have mentioned so far, a statement like "kill them wherever you may find them," which actually refers to a very special and conditional situation, is prone to be misperceived as permission for some people with violent tendencies to satisfy themselves. This statement is, again, in the context of the battlefield where combatants are in a live-or-die situation. Muslims are told in this verse

---

6   Al-Baqarah, 194, 217; al-Maedah, 2, 97; at-Tawbah, 36.

to do whatever they must not to die and to be victorious. This verse in no way refers to all polytheists living in Muslim or non-Muslim lands; such an interpretation is possible only if we detach this verse from the context of the set of verses with which it is found. Likewise, it does not refer to any polytheist who lives in Muslim lands who does not take any aggressive attitude towards Muslims and who supports peace and coexistence. Polytheists who are not in a combatant position are also excluded. To repeat, this verse is about Meccan polytheists who adopted a certain attitude by venturing into war, ignored all diplomatic attempts for peace, betrayed treaties, and became—in political and legal terms—a combatant. There are some jurists, however, who take this verse as binding in all circumstances and for all polytheists. Extremist groups in our time prefer to adopt their views on this, for it suits their interests.

If we consider the group of verses in terms of its purpose and wisdom, we understand that killing is not the sole and ultimate option. The Qur'an makes frequent reference to peace and good relations in different contexts. So, the verse in question must be considered in a frame of principles in accordance with the general wisdom and purposes of the Qur'an. Otherwise, such verses will be prone to be abused for justifying the violent tendencies of marginal groups. Let us never overlook the fact that all such verses with heavy judgments pertain to exceptional situations.

Considering the overall revelatory process of the Qur'an and its general purposes, we can confidently argue that no single verse contains any material, symbolic, or psychological tool that can be abused by murderers to satisfy themselves. It is impossible to reach extremist views out of these verses unless one completely ignores the Qur'an's general purposes and wisdom that are based on reason and relatable to human beings at the individual and social levels. This is what some marginal groups are doing to legitimize their actions by overstretching traditional tools of exposition (*ta'lil*), methodology (*usul*), and exegesis (*tafsir*). Islam counsels believers not to give in to their emotions but to take their feelings under control and be mindful of certain principles even in the heat of war: actions like going to extremes in fighting, using disproportionate force, killing non-combatants, torturing captives, mutilating corpses, and even harming trees and the land; other such atrocities are also forbidden. These are not mere pieces of advice; the Qur'an commands Muslims to obey these rules.

Right after the command "kill them," the verse continues to count other possible options and mentions catching and imprisoning them. This clearly demonstrates that there are open-ended options to be practiced according to practical circumstances. The following expressions about surrounding them and blocking the ways they may pass support our argument that killing is not the sole option.

What really matters here is preventing the offensive behaviors of the polytheists. The *fazlaka* of the verse also supports this:

> However, if they repent, surrender to Islam, and observe due responsibilities, open their ways and leave them alone. Undoubtedly, God is oft-forgiving of sins, and has abundant mercy and compassion for His servants who turn to Him repentantly.

In conclusion, like the thinker Ali Bulaç says, the command to kill here needs to be taken like a commander giving the order to fire at war and then continuing to act in accordance with the rules of warfare.[7] I would like to underline once more that according to the meaning drawn from the context and overall purpose of the verses, killing at war is not the prime option but the last one. What matters is not killing the enemy in the absolute sense but killing for not being killed. If you are able to realize "not being killed" without killing the other—for example if you can neutralize and imprison your enemies without killing them, then you should do so. Or if it is possible to maintain an environment of peace and security by other means, then these should be given priority. There is no exclusive way, option, or attitude to "kill!" no matter what.

The verb "*qatl*" (to kill) is mentioned in the Qur'an hundreds of times in all its derivative forms. However, it is used in the imperative only in three instances, all of which are in the context of war. In addition, as we mentioned while evaluating the verses from chapter al-Baqarah, some scholars declaring that other verses related to making agreements and approaching others with tolerance are abrogated is not correct according to the purpose of the general principles of the Qur'an. Based on the exegetical principle "particularity of the causes of revela-

---

7   Ali Bulaç, *Kur'an Dersleri* [Qur'an Lessons], Vol. 1, p. 415.

tion (*asbab al-nuzul*) does not prevent drawing a general principle or judgment from it," some even include all polytheists who will live until the end of the world. Such an overgeneralization is neither compatible with the teachings of the Qur'an nor with those of the noble Prophet. This exegetical principle is an important rule; however, it should not be instrumentalized by anybody as they please just to legitimize their intentions and purposes.

It is a noteworthy fact that despite the polytheists' years of tormenting Muslims, the verse reveals that the door of repentance was still open to them, which is a sign of divine mercy. Normally, it is not easy to accept the fact that brutal polytheists are given an opportunity to start with a clean sheet after all they had done to the Muslims. It would not be surprising if any Muslim reacted with a sense of revenge after years of persecution, betrayal, and exile. Yet, the Muslims did not give any negative reaction. On the day of the conquest of Mecca, the noble Prophet declared a general amnesty for the polytheists of Mecca; he said to them, "No reproach shall be on you today..." He preferred the way of tolerance, and the Muslims who had been hurt in every way did not make the slightest objection. Can this be ascribed to a strict strategy of war and killing? On the contrary, this was nothing but an affirmation of the peaceful, humane, and ethical conduct brought by Qur'anic teaching.

At this point, it is worth considering reasons this verse was named the "verse of the sword" by some scholars of exegesis, as well as the unintended consequences of this naming. Probably, when this phrase was first used, people did not think it would pave the way for abuse by some groups; it was a simple reference to the fact that the verse mentioned killing. On the other hand, this phrase may have been coined to denote a very exceptional situation.

Whatever the reasons may be, this verse is not the only basis radical groups rely on to support their pro-war policies. This verse may provide psychological support for their actions, but there are multiple political and socio-cultural factors at the international level that result in acts of violence. In other words, seeing the issue of emerging radical groups solely as a consequence of rigid interpretation of religious texts does not comply with the realities. Even in their declared discourses, they put insistent emphasis on colonialism, cultural hegemony of the West, and societal degeneration caused by modernity. It is possible to make a longer list, but the purpose of this book is not to give all the reasons of marginal causes of violence but to study how these groups misinterpret Islamic literature, especially certain Qur'anic verses, including this so-called "verse of the sword."

Technically, some commentators may have preferred an extensive range of meaning and considered that the verse could be generalized to encompass all polytheists to come until the Last Day. Suggesting alternative meanings and comments can be understandable within scholarly discussions despite the possible ramifications of marginal commentaries. Just as the existence of marginal intellectual ideas in philosophy do not necessitate a total negation of the entire philosophical tradition, the same holds true for marginal opinions and commentaries about the Islamic tradition of exegesis. Although they remain marginal, a limited number of scholars did claim that this verse about declaring war abrogated many verses about peace and good relations in the Qur'an. But, as we expressed before, a holistic textual consideration refutes such comments. Taking this verse – which refers to Meccan polytheists who broke their agreement – as the sole criterion will mean disregarding other ones making statements as follows:

> There is no coercion in religion. (al-Baqarah 2:256)

> Call to the way of your Lord with wisdom and fair exhortation. (an-Nahl 16:125)

> God does not forbid you, as regards those who do not make war against you on account of your Religion, nor drive you away from your homes, to be kindly to them, and act towards them with equity. (al-Mumtahana 60:8)

> And by no means let your detestation for a people (or their detestation for you) move you to (commit the sin of) deviating from justice. Be just: this is nearer and more suited to righteousness and piety. (al-Maedah 5:8)

While there are many such verses in this respect, disregarding these verses and the principles they teach conflicts with the spirit of

Islam. Going further and taking an extremist commentary as basis as a way to eliminate these principles means the utter destruction of Islam. Even the fact that those who did not breach the treaty are excepted is sufficient for dismissing extremist comments.

At-Tawbah 9:6

Seeking asylum

> And if any of those (Meccans) who associate partners with God seeks asylum of you (O Messenger), grant him asylum, so that he may hear the Word of God, and then convey him to his place of security (without betraying your promise for security about life and property). That (is how you should act) because they are a people who have no knowledge (of the truth about Islam).

Many translations of this verse consider "who associate partners with God" in the beginning of this verse in its absolute meaning to refer to all polytheists. Considering the verse with the reason of revelation and its context, it is possible to see that it actually refers to the Meccan polytheists. I preferred to add (Meccan) in the translation above to clarify the authentic meaning of the verse and not to leave any gaps for overgeneralizations in its meaning.

If we look at the issue from a broader perspective, in addition to 1) accepting Islam, 2) leaving Mecca, or 3) warring, this verse is offering another option to Meccan polytheists: *aman*, or seeking asylum. Asylum is when a government assures the protection of life and property.

To whom, then, does the Qur'an give the right to seek asylum? According to some scholars, this right is for polytheists who are unaware of the developments mentioned thus far. According to another opinion, it is valid for those who do not have definite enmity against Muslims and remain neutral—who do not want to take part in fighting neither against their own people nor Muslims.[8] Verse 90 of chapter an-Nisa is important in terms of showing such people's presence: "Except those

8   Ali Bulaç, *Kur'an Dersleri* [Qur'an Lessons], 3/407.

who seek refuge in a people between whom and you there is a treaty (of peace or alliance), or (those who) come to you with hearts shrinking from fighting against you, as well as fighting against their own people. Had God willed, He would certainly have given them power over you and they would have fought against you. If they withdraw from you and do not fight against you, and offer you peace, then God allows you no way (to war) against them."

According to some other scholars, the people referred to are those who bear doubts about Islam, as stated in, "so that he (or they) may hear the Word of God..." And according to yet another scholarly opinion, which I also agree with, the verse refers to the entirety of the polytheists of Mecca. This is the one that suits the spirit of Islam best. Accordingly, instead of condemning all polytheists straightly, those who wish to learn about Islam are given an opportunity, and they are provided with security of life and property as a suitable ground for thinking about religion.

Let us assume that they did not decide to accept Islam in the end; then how are they to be treated? As the verse does not invalidate the right to asylum granted to them, it also lets them be rendered to a place of safety. When considered from this regard, the asylum option granted to the polytheists also eliminates the possibility of coercion to accept religion. Otherwise, if the polytheists said for example, "We neither abandon Mecca, nor make war," then accepting Islam would be the only remaining option. And this would give them the excuse to say, "we were pressured and coerced to accept Islam."

The phrase "so that he may hear the Word of God" is a part of the Qur'an's theological language; it would not be an accurate understanding to connect religious reasons to seeking asylum. Of course, it is very important to enable the polytheists to think about Islam free from any pressure and feelings of animosity and weigh it against his or her own faith—and this is what this verse is laying the groundwork for. Then, we can argue that the right to seek asylum is not intended in this verse as a tool for forced choice but as a more humane approach. In short, granting the Meccan polytheists the option to seek asylum is a historical and practical example of "freedom of religion and conscience," to put it in contemporary language.

At-Tawbah 9:7

Encouraging an ethical attitude

> How could there be a covenant with those (Meccans) who associate
> partners with God (and recognize no laws and treaty) on the part of
> God and His Messenger? – excepting those with whom you made
> a treaty (such as the Kinanah and Damirah tribes) in the vicinity of
> the Sacred Mosque: (as for the latter) so long as they remain true to
> you, be true to them. Surely God loves believers who are God-rever-
> ing and pious (who reverently observe the boundaries He set, who
> refrain from breaching their treaty, who keep away from sins and act
> with a responsibility of being a servant of God, who act honorably
> and defend their rights and freedoms, and who are aware of their
> religious and social duties).

When the verse is read carefully, it will be seen that it covers almost everything mentioned from the beginning of the chapter until
here. In a way, it eliminates all possibilities that may come to the mind
of the Prophet's Companions. For example, even though a four-month
respite is given, the ultimatum given to the polytheists of Mecca can at
first sight appear as a practice that conflicts with the general Islamic
teachings to date. The Meccans had committed lots of treacherous acts
against the Muslims, and some of the Prophet's Companions could potentially object to being so lenient with them.

The verse warns Muslims to be cautious of people who are not
faithful to their words. For, such people keep changing their direction
depending on their interests. When such people represent a tribe, a nation, or a state, Muslims should be extra careful. Being deceived at that
level of representation could bring fatal consequences to the future of
Islam. Offering so many options to such unreliable polytheists was not
something to digest easily for many Muslims. It was an incredible manifestation of sacrifice and submission by the Companions of the Prophet
that they accepted the rulings of the verse despite the fact they suffered
from and witnessed all the atrocities committed by the polytheists. It
would have been quite normal if the Muslims demanded the polytheists

face all the consequences of their crimes. The Qur'anic verses, however, commanded a more humane and ethical behavior.

After verse 7 points out the polytheists cannot have a covenant with God and His Messenger anymore, it states an exception for those "who have not failed to fulfill their obligations" in verse 4 once more, eliminating any misunderstandings. With reference to those who observed the treaty, verse 7 continues: "so long as they remain true to you, be true to them. Surely God loves the God-revering, pious (who keep their duties to Him)." Thus, the importance of being faithful to a promise is emphasized again. According to the information related in works of exegesis, the people referred to were the Damrah and Kinanah tribes, who did not show any hostility towards the Muslims after the treaty was made.

Let us elucidate two points here: Firstly, the treaty mentioned as "near the Sacred Mosque" is the Treaty of Hudaybiyah. The treaty was referred to thusly since the Sacred Mosque was regarded as sacred by both sides. Secondly, the tribe that signed the Hudaybiyah Treaty was the leading tribe, the Quraysh. Considering the tribal system of the period, there were sub-tribes affiliated with the Quraysh; they were regarded as accepting every treaty the Quraysh made. The incident that caused the invalidation of the Hudaybiyah Treaty was the fact that a tribe (the Banu Duil of the Banu Bakr) allied with the Quraysh attacked a tribe (the Huzaa) allied with the Muslims. As for the tribes of the Bani Kinanah and Banu Damrah excepted by the verse, they did nothing to breach the treaty. Note that, these two lesser tribes could have normally been under the coverage of the ultimatum according to the customs of Arab society of the time because of their affiliation with the Quraysh, but they were excepted by the Qur'an for their non-hostile attitude.[9]

Secondly, Muslims were at the height of their power and could have preferred to take revenge for the past 22 years of torture, exile, and oppression. But this would contradict their faith, ethical values, and principles of law. As a matter of fact, the word *muttaqi* (God-revering and pious) in the end statement of the verse emphasizes that acting with justice and moderation is more ideal in piety. Even though this phrase is not in the form of a commandment, the expected attitude is clearly expressed.

---

9   See Hamdi Yazir 4/279.

At-Tawbah 9:8

Attributes of the polytheists against whom war is declared

> How else could it be (How could there be a covenant with the others)?—when, if they were to prevail against you, they would observe towards you neither any bond, nor law, nor agreement. They seek to please you with their mouths, but in their hearts they are averse; and most of them are transgressors (who habitually disregard all bounds of equity).

The expression which we translated as "How else could it be?" could be rendered in a very literal and thus obscure way as, "How?" This is the preference in some works of translation, but it would cause a loss of a nuance. This group of verses from 7 to 12 portrays the polytheists of Mecca in terms of their character, inner worlds, and the negative intentions they bore against Muslims. Accordingly, those people who were full of rage, grudge, and hatred were not expected to remain faithful to the covenant they had made with the Muslims. So, they would either forsake polytheism and become Muslim, or abandon Mecca—a land of monotheism—or they would be fought against. There was no other way; this was what Meccans wanted with all of their animosity against Muslims for 22 years.

At-Tawbah 9:9-10

> (9) (As well as breaking their treaties) they have sold God's Revelations (concerning treaties) for a trifling price and they barred people from His way. How evil is what they do! (10) When the rights of a believer are concerned, those polytheists observe neither any bond, nor law, nor responsibility for their agreement. They are those (rampant antagonists who recognize no rights and) who exceed all bounds.

The brilliant scholar of exegesis Hamdi Yazır made a beautiful commentary on these verses:

> The statement in the verse reflects a complete negativity (*salb al-kulli*), which means that polytheists do not recognize anything as

agreement or liability. Namely, if they find an opportunity, they neither recognize God, nor their oath, nor bonds, nor their agreement nor any obligation. They have no concern about the most significant liabilities; they ferociously do away with you in broad daylight and do whatever they like.

In sum, they do not observe any Divine or human rights whatsoever.

"They seek to please you with their mouths…" They pay lip service to faith, friendship, humanity, and fairness; they even take oaths for the sake of credibility. When what they do turns out to be the opposite of what they say, they make apologies with baseless excuses. However, they do so through their teeth and their hearts do not support such meaning. The words in their mouth are in utter conflict with the intention in their hearts.

"(As well as breaking their treaties) they have sold God's Revelations (concerning treaties) for a trifling price and they barred people from His way." They tried to blockade the way to the Ka'ba, to avert people from worship and prayer to God. It was reported that once Abu Sufyan, the leader of Mecca, gave a feast for his own supporters only, excluding those who sided with the Prophet. Tempted by something as simple as food, some broke their word to the Muslims.

The verse continues as "They observe neither any bond, nor law, nor agreement towards the believers." That is, they neither observe the rights of believers in general nor those of a single person.

"They are those who exceed all bounds." Such are the very persons against whom the appropriate ultimatum and warning for war was given because they were the ones who actually continued their aggressive attitude.[10]

At-Tawbah 9:11

An emphasis on brotherhood despite everything

Yet if they (polytheists of Mecca) repent so as to mend their ways and establish the Prescribed Prayer and pay the Prescribed Puri-

---

10   See, Hamdi Yazir, 4/280.

fying Alms, they are your brothers in religion. Thus We set out in detail Our Revelations (the signposts of Our way, included in the Qur'an) for a people seeking knowledge.

By stating that the door to repentance is always open, the verse highlights a very important point: A person cannot live forever with the consciousness of being guilty. No matter how gross their sin is, there must always be an open door, which is repentance. Surely, there can also be certain punishments in the literal sense if a wrong committed amounts to a crime. Otherwise, there would remain no justice or societal order. What really matters is to develop a feeling of remorse within and choose to shift to a virtuous and ethical life. Without such a possibility of change, this is likely to lead to a more complicated, psychological, and pathological consequence. Leaving a door open to remorse and repentance is important for a person's belief and points to a humane situation at the societal level.

A second point is that a person is a being potentially open to changes and transformation. People can object to what they affirmed yesterday or affirm tomorrow what they reject today. Mostly, they are able to assert arguments for such change with reference to their thoughts and feelings. Although this change can be for the negative in some cases, the development of human potential is mostly dependent on this ability for change and adaptation. Human life does not solely consist of rights—in many instances, it proceeds with mistakes. What is right more often than not becomes clearer after painful experiences of doing wrong. A person moves forward after having learned their lesson after many missteps, trials, and errors. Giving this opportunity to Meccan polytheists despite all the evil they committed shows God's expansive mercy and compassion, as much as it shows that this mercy and compassion are in the best interest of individuals and society.

Not only in this verse, but in many other chapters does the Qur'an point to the human inclination to sin, err, and antagonize—and conversely to their potential to learn and turn to virtuous living. Be that as it may, were Muslims ready to accept this condition, especially given the fact that war was commanded against the Meccan polytheists who persecuted them in all possible ways and breached their treaty? Supposing that the polytheists did choose to accept Islam, would the Muslims

welcome the malefactors who had put them through a prolonged ordeal?

The Qur'an commands that they do so: on the condition of ceas-
ing their oppression, accepting Islam, observing the daily prayers, and
giving the *zakat* alms, the Qur'an describes the polytheists as "your
brothers." "Your brothers" is the farthest possible expression of acceptance to eliminate vengeful feelings that might arise.

Many of the Muslims themselves were polytheists not so long before. After they embraced Islam, they decided to mend their ways, by
observing prayer for one God together with their fellow believers and
became engaged with society by means of the alms (*zakat*); they gained
a different character and identity.

The same opportunity for this psychological transformation was
now being given to other polytheists as well. Since many among the
Muslims had already experienced this transformation, they would be
expected to show consent; together with that, the verse takes it further.
Considering the word "brother" and the effect it has on a person's spirit
and heart, the expected psychological transformation was consolidat-
ed with a stronger and deeper essential. Verse 10 of chapter al-Huju-
rat—"The believers are but brothers"—can be cited as more evidence
that supports this feeling. Islam, like all heavenly religions, supports this
sense of a brotherly society.

Let us consider the possibility of an extreme: what if the polytheists who broke their treaty and who were given a new chance broke
their word again and returned to their old habits? The verse continues
to reveal the ultimate act against such possibility and states that "...But
if they (polytheists of Mecca) break their pledges after their treaty (with
you) and assail your Religion, then fight with those leaders of unbelief—
surely they have no trustworthy pledges—so that they may desist (from
aggression). It is hoped that as a result of your fighting back, they give
up their assaults to you and to your religion."

I would also like to point out that the end statement of verse 11
means, "...We set out in detail Our Revelations for a people seeking
knowledge." In this context, the meaning of the verse and the message it
gives to humanity are very clear: these verses are not meant for people
who do not think and try to understand, who do not ponder over verses
and their wisdoms; on the contrary, they are for those who think, who

understand, and who at least try to understand them. Then, the Qur'an means to say, you go beyond imitating others in faith; investigate these verses, ponder over the reasons and wisdom of the commandments and prohibitions, and practice them accordingly.

On the other hand, we see that even in the situation of a warfare, the Qur'an still invites people to accept faith and addresses sound reason and common sense. Similar calls for people to ponder are made at the end of so many end statements (*fazlaka*). The Qur'an sometimes directly addresses the human intellect by using strong phrases like, "do you not ever think?" and points to the "lessons to learn for those who reason." Many of the emphases at the end of chapters come in reference to Divine names and attributes—sometimes apparently outside the context of revelation, but in a form that constructs a supra-language to idealize a more humane, ethical, and virtuous attitude that surpasses the situation at hand. This is the Qur'an's general style of invitation that encourages people to seek virtuous behavior and lofty ideals. If human nature did not have a capacity to seek and reach that ethical perfection, the Qur'an would not have this much emphasis on these ideals. In short, the teachings of Islamic revelation target societal life with the aim of developing within peace, mutual respect, sound reason, and common sense. This is why verses in the Qur'an frequently end by establishing a relationship between Divine wisdoms, human reason, and common sense.

At-Tawbah 9:12

Leaders of unbelief

> ...But if they (polytheists of Mecca) break their pledges after their
> treaty (with you) and assail your Religion, then fight with those
> leaders of unbelief—surely they have no trustworthy pledges (it has
> no validity anymore)—so that they may desist (from aggression).

Since the verse is referring here to the polytheists who broke their treaty, we can understand this verse as re-emphasizing the attitude to be taken against them, along with citing the reasons for war. According to this, a unilateral violation of a peace agreement is a reason for war until a new agreement is made.

The second reason for war stated by the verse is assailing religion or abusive talk against religion. This assault is considered to be physical obstruction of and enmity against religious freedom. Otherwise, expressing one's thoughts about the values of other religions or propagating one's own religion falls within the freedom of religion—as long as they do not pressure or coerce others in this regard and do not engage in abusive talk. Physical obstructions are deemed a reason for war.

Another point that draws attention here is the expression "leaders of unbelief"; this does not refer to a few people who led the polytheists but the Meccan polytheists who breached the treaty and are being addressed by the ultimatum. This meaning gains priority when we consider the context and coherence of text. Indeed, when we consider the issue from the historical perspective, we see that it was Meccan polytheists who took the lead at persecuting and tormenting the Muslims during the 13 years in Mecca before the Muslims had to emigrate.

An alternative meaning, especially considering the outward form of the phrase, may be referring to the governing elite who led the polytheists. Or it can be read as a measure against those who organize and lead physical assaults against freedom of faith. Since a decision for war does not lie with individuals but with state authorities, it is obvious that the pro-war Meccan polytheist leaders are being referenced here.

In any given society, some individuals might commit verbal or physical attacks against religious freedoms. The lawful response to such attacks needs to take into consideration freedoms of thought and expression.

The thinker Ali Bulaç makes the following commentary:

> For historical, religious, and political reasons, some societies can
> be bearing feelings of animosity against others. However, societies
> generally act under the directives of those who govern them; they
> adopt the character of their leader. As the phrase goes, "the people
> follow the religion of their king." Governing elites make use of the
> influential means in their hands and indoctrinate societies. They
> build hostile perceptions and seek to gain some geo-strategic and
> political advantages by triggering feelings of animosity. A war de-
> clared for the reasons stated in the two verses (12 and 13) is in a way

a war declared against the leaders of the opposing society. Another possible meaning can be a reference to a group within the opposing society, especially some persons and circles who went to extremes at enmity and torment against Muslims. Not everybody shows hostility of the same degree; some might have more rancor and take their aggression to excessive degrees and destruction. The scholar Qurtubi comments that even if they do not have the position of a leader, those who break the treaty and engage in abusive talk are assumed to be in a leading position in this respect, and the verse commands making war against such people.[11]

If we consider the concept of "abusive talk against religion" with historical realities, it can be interpreted as insulting religion and religious values on the one hand and posing a barrier before the freedom of faith and preventing people from choosing Islam with their free will on the other. As is known, in addition to their attacks, the polytheists of Mecca did their best to fill with hatred those who had no prior knowledge of Islam.

Concerning the statement in the verse whose translation we gave as, "they have no trustworthy pledges (they have no validity anymore)," the late authority of Qur'anic exegesis Hamdi Yazır makes the following noteworthy commentary:

> For them (polytheists), there is nothing to pledge for. There is no place for any sacred value in their hearts. Since there is no place, meaning, or value for a pledge/oath in their hearts, they make a pledge merely with their mouths. No matter how seriously they seem to take an oath with their mouths, it is vain, too. They do not observe the pledge they took. Since they do not believe in an oath, they don't see anything wrong with breaking it. Their having no place for an oath is understood from the degree of their excess at their denial. It is impossible to have an oath or treaty with them anymore. Making a treaty with them depends on their being saved from (the vice of) their recognizing no oaths. And this can only be possible by making war against them because such extremists do not understand from anything but brutal force. They do not come to

---

11   Ali Bulaç, *Kur'ân Dersleri* [Qur'an Lessons], 3/482.

their senses any other way. For this reason, declare war against those unbelievers who recognize no treaties, so that they give that up. So that they put a stop to their abusive talk against your religion, stop recognizing no treaties and stop continually breaching them. Namely, declare war against them with the intent and motive of making them to recognize law. This should be your real purpose for fighting against them. Otherwise, let it not be merely for inflicting harm to the opposite side, let it not be for harassing and killing them, as commonly done by aggressors.[12]

As it will also be seen from the commentary of Yazır, the main purpose here is to put a stop to abusive talk and acts against Muslims by the leaders of unbelief; the purpose is not making war at all. If they give up their lawless attitude, then there is no point in fighting. The ending of the verse, "so that they may desist (from aggression)" also indicates this clearly. However, in any case, a decision for war is something that occurs between two legitimate states; it is a political and legal decision on an international level taken after mutual or unilateral acts of aggression. Acts of aggression may refer to any form of animosity against sacred values, symbols of independence, political authority, and economic resources. Declaring war against individuals is not something that can be deduced from this verse. Individuals should be cautioned with argumentation and legal action. If the verse is interpreted to include declaring war against individuals—which would be an interpretation that does not take historical context into consideration—then this would allow room for legitimizing radical commentaries that consider disbelief and polytheism as reasons for war. The decision to make war is enough as evidence that such a commentary would be false.

At-Tawbah 9:13
Responding to war with war

(O believers!) Will you not fight against the people who have broken their pledges and have done all they could to drive the Messenger

---

12   Hamdi Yazır, 4/282.

(from where he chooses to dwell), and (they were the ones who)
initiated hostilities against you? Do you hold them in awe? But,
assuredly God has greater right to be held in awe, if you are sincere
believers.

The verse encourages Muslims to make war against the polytheists
who did not leave the Muslims with any other option but war. The polytheists not only violated their treaty and forced the Muslims to exile, but
most importantly, they started the war first. Before the Muslims' emigration to Medina, polytheists had inflicted various torments and tor-
tures on believers. Later, they even made an offensive campaign, which
resulted in the Battle of Badr. One year later, they came again in the
Battle of Uhud and then made one more offensive with the Battle of the
Trench. Afterwards, they did not allow Muslims who had come for pilgrimage into Mecca. They signed the Treaty of Hudaybiyah, which was
all in their favor, but they did not comply with it. Considering the Hunayn campaign, the polytheists were the side who started the offensive
again. By taking advantage of the Tabuk campaign where Muslims tried
to stop the advance of the Romans, they caused much trouble against
the Muslims. The only way to stop them was war.

What did the Muslims do in response to all of these atrocities?
They responded with patience, as history verifies. They did not trans-
gress any legal or moral boundaries. But in the end, war was the last,
only solution. The Muslims would not fear war; they were not supposed
to fear anyone but God. The verse already makes this point without any
need for further interpretation: "Do you hold them in awe? But, assuredly God has greater right to be held in awe, if you are sincere believers."

Right at this point, the following question may come to mind:
"What is actually meant by war?" Is it only defeating the enemy and
putting an end to their oppression, or does a possible victory hold other advantages for Muslims? The following verses, verses 14-16, answer
these questions.

At-Tawbah 9:14-16

(O believers!) Fight against them: God will punish them by your
hands and humiliate them, and (know) that He will help you to

victory over them, and soothe the bosoms of the believing people (oppressed and suffering at their hands, as well as at the hands of other oppressors). And He will remove the wrath in their hearts (by making right and justice prevail). And God guides whomever He wills to turn to Him in repentance. God is All-Knowing (with full knowledge of him who deserves guidance), All-Wise (in Whose every decree and act there are many instances of wisdom). Or did you think that you would be left (without being tried through suffering and hardship) unless God marks out those among you who really strive (in His way), and who take none as intimate friend other than God and His Messenger and the believers to seek help and solidarity? God is fully aware of all that you do.

These verses emphasize that the actual point of war is not revenge. Seeking revenge does not comply with faith, ethics, virtue, and fairness. In this respect, Islam brought certain new principles and bans—which we can summarize as legal and ethical rules for warfare—which did not previously exist in Arab society.

All of these principles are a body of values intertwined with humane, moral, and religious aspects: not killing non-combatants such as women, children, elderly, clergy, and envoys; not mutilating corpses; not committing rape; and not harming the environment among them. These bans and regulations sought to prevent atrocities and minimize the psychological and material harms of war. In addition to not harming the elderly, women, children, ascetics devoted to worship, and temples, the Prophet instructed Muslims to not burn trees, not harm animals, and not destroy wealth.[13] Mutilation of corpses was a common practice in pre-Islamic times.

Returning to the verse again, in the face of a great toll the war brings, the verse reminds Muslims of an important principle of faith and submission: "God will punish them by your hands." Accordingly, Muslims fight, die, suffer, and pay a high price during the war, but God is the actual punisher. This refers to the central theme of *tawhid* in Islam—that everything is possible only with the permission of God, Who is in possession of all power and possibilities. Muslims are expected to

---

13   Ahmad ibn Hanbal, Musnad 1/300; Abu Dawud, Jihad 90, 121.

observe *tawhid* in all their actions and with the consciousness that they will account for everything they do in this life.

Secondly, if the war results in victory, Muslims are not supposed to take any personal pride, for victory would not be possible without God's permission and support. Normally, their faith already sets an obstacle to self-pride, but faith may not reveal its sanctioning power without firm ethical foundations and modes of behavior.

Considering the points made in this verse, "God will punish them by your hands and humiliate them, and (know) that He will help you to victory over them, and soothe the bosoms of the believing people," almost all scholars of exegesis agreed that these points refer to the incident that caused the invalidation of the peace treaty of Hudaybiyah: the Banu Bakr tribe, allied with the Quraysh, attacked Banu Huzaa, allied with the Muslims. They killed a few people, and some polytheists of Mecca helped them. Afterwards, with the Conquest of Mecca and the victory of Hunayn, the enemies were punished, the safety of believers was maintained, and law-and-order was re-established. The verse firstly talks about this incident.

From a broader perspective, all Muslims have been declared brothers and sisters. Faith makes a stronger bond among them than their blood relations. In reference to this bond, the Prophet says, "As regards their being merciful among themselves and showing love among themselves and being kind, you see the believers resembling one body, so that if any part of the body is not well then the whole body shares the sleeplessness (insomnia) and fever with it."[14] Thus, the success and joy of believers in one place make believers all over the world happy and brings comfort to their souls. The late Hamdi Yazır comments on this verse and states that there are five different wisdoms in war, which must be considered altogether. He draws attention to the fact that meeting only one of these but failing to meet others will mean not observing the war law, and that this might deepen mutual hatred and pave the way for further wars:

1. Retribution against the unjust
2. To neutralize the offenders and eliminate the danger

---

14   Bukhari, Adab, 27; Muslim, Birr, 66.

3. To honor believers

4. To bring comfort to the persecuted believers

5. To establish justice, and thus leave no place for both sides to seek vengeance."[15]

The verse continues as follows: "[God] will remove the wrath in their hearts (by making right and justice prevail). And God guides whomever He wills to turn to Him in repentance." The question of whom this verse addresses has been a matter of discussion among scholars throughout history. It is thought that the verse can either be addressing Muslims who underwent an ordeal and persecution, and who later were engaged in thoughts and acts unbecoming for believers; or it can be addressing leading unbelievers like Abu Sufyan, Ikrima ibn Abu Jahl, or Suhayl ibn Amr, who later repented and accepted Islam.

The statement of the verse and its relation to the following and prior verses, together with the reason for revelation clearly demonstrates that the second meaning is more likely. Muslims who had been subjected to their atrocities could bear vengeful feelings, see the latter's accepting faith as expedient, and attempt to avenge themselves when they found the opportunity. It is possible that with this statement, the verse warns Muslims against such possible negative thoughts and acts. This meaning is supported by the following *fazlaka*: "God is All-Knowing (with full knowledge of him who deserves guidance), All-Wise (in Whose every decree and act there are many instances of wisdom)."

Some scholars of exegesis favor the first possibility and suggest that this address is to Muslims. Some Muslims may not have understood the wisdom of what happened and might have been holding negative feelings about the trials they endured. Therefore, the verse can indeed be addressing Muslims, too. After referring to general attitude and behaviors about war, verse 16 states:

> Or did you think that you would be left (without being tried
> through suffering and hardship) unless God marks out those among
> you who really strive (in His way), and who take none as intimate

---

15   Hamdi Yazır, 4/285-286.

friend other than God and His Messenger and the believers to seek help and solidarity? God is fully aware of all that you do.

Thus, believers are supposed to live with the consciousness that this world is a trial ground, that their actions are under the surveillance of the omnipresent Creator, and that they must act responsibly in every way. Wars, diseases, and tribulations of every material or spiritual kind are traumatic situations. They are the acid test of character weaknesses in people. On the other hand, they can also be a means of personal development. If people are going through a test, then they are on the way to progress. People who never face any difficulties are not likely to improve their character. So, the verse cautions believers by underlining the fact that war and similar conditions might have a traumatic impact on behavior and belief. In order to reveal how people will use their potential, the Divine Will subjects them to various difficulties. This is a Divine principle, and the verse points out this wisdom explicitly. One cannot help but agree with the following commentary by the thinker Ali Bulaç, concerning verses 12-16:

> War is not made for the sake of war. The reason for war is eliminating injustice and oppression, preventing offenders, and punishing those who try to violate others' land, wealth, and chastity. Maintaining freedom of faith and conscience and providing people with a dignified life is among the wise purposes targeted. However, the aggressive, ambitious, and oppressors will always oppose this; so war is necessary in such cases. People are not on their own in this world; there are certain moral and social responsibilities they must observe. The purpose of a righteous war is differentiating those who sincerely observe these responsibilities from others… The fact that whenever fighting is mentioned in the Qur'an, it comes with a condition to be "in the way of God," is for emphasizing that the only lawful purpose of war and struggle must be seeking God's good pleasure. Therefore, wars and struggles made out of personal, familial, group-based, national, ethnical, or regional concerns and benefits are "excluded" from the notion of "fighting in the way of God." Those who target political, material, and other worldly gains are not considered to have fought in the way of God. As a general rule, unbelievers seek the friendship of those who are like themselves. Sometimes, they

seem to be among believers in a hypocritical sense, but war is a factor that reveals a person's true character.[16]

The verses that follow begin by answering some possible questions that may arise in the minds of Muslims. This can be the case in societal life. Some people are probably discussing them quietly, or at least considering them within. In his commentary Izzat Darwaza relates this verse's reason for revelation. Accordingly, some discussed whether polytheists would receive a reward from God for providing the services for pilgrims. Polytheists also used the Ka'ba as a place of worship and regarded it as sacred. Therefore, the honorable duties such as maintenance of the Ka'ba (*imara*), and providing water for pilgrims (*siqaya*), were granted to certain tribes, which was a matter of prestige between them; they would compete to undertake these duties and those who carried them out for centuries would boast about it. Although there were other duties of pilgrimage, the mention of only these two in the 19th verse affirms the reason for revelation given by Darwaza. We will quote his explanations after giving a translation of the verse group from 17 to 22, which have a clear content of meaning when considered altogether.

At-Tawbah 9:17-22
Integrity of faith, intention, and deeds

It is not for those who associate partners with God to maintain God's houses of worship while they are witnesses against themselves of unbelief (and do not worship God in those houses of worship). They are those whose works (of maintaining the Ka'ba) have been wasted, and they will abide in the Fire. (17)

Only he will maintain God's houses of worship (using them for the purposes for which they are built) who believes in God and the Last Day, and establishes the prayer, and pays the alms, and stands in awe of none but God. It is hoped that such (illustrious) persons will be

16   Ali Bulaç, *Kur'an Dersleri*, [Qur'an Lessons] 3/485.

among the ones guided to achieve their expectations (especially in the Hereafter). (18)

Do you consider providing water to the pilgrims and tending the Sacred Mosque as equal in value to one who believes in God and the Last Day, and strives in God's cause? They are not equal in God's sight. And God does not guide (to truth) the wrongdoing folk (whose measure and judgment are wrong). (19)

Those who believe and have emigrated (to the home of Islam in God's cause), and strive in God's cause with their wealth and persons are greater in rank in God's sight, and those are the ones who are the triumphant. (20)

Their Lord gives them glad tidings of mercy from Him (to bring unforeseen blessings), and His being pleased with them, and of Gardens wherein is everlasting bounty for them. (21)

Therein to dwell forever. Surely, with God is a tremendous reward. (22)

Verses 17, 18, and 19 mention the pilgrimage services for the Ka'ba and its visitors, which also existed in pre-Islamic Arab society, with a particular emphasis on the structure's maintenance and providing water for pilgrims.

A second thing to consider in these three verses is the phrase "God's places of worship," used when the subject matter is the Ka'ba.

The third thing is the comparison made in verse 19, which clearly states that the pilgrimage services are not as virtuous as faith in God and the Day of Judgment and struggling in the way of God. According to the report by Numan ibn Bashir, the following case is the reason for revelation:

On a Friday, three people were exchanging opinions about an issue in the Prophet's Mosque. One of them said, that the most important deed in his sight was providing water for pilgrims. Another disagreed and remarked that maintenance of the Sacred Mosque was more meritorious. The third one stated his opinion that struggling in the way of

God and His Messenger was better than these two. In the end, Umar ibn al-Khattab warned them by saying, "do not raise your voices near the pulpit of God's Messenger," so they stopped the discussion.

Numan ibn Bashir said:

> "After the Prayer, I went near the Messenger of God and asked about the right answer for the issue on which they disagreed. Upon this, the relevant verse was revealed."[17]

According to the historical sources, particular pilgrimage services did exist prior to Islam, and their scope was clear. Each of these services would be fulfilled by certain tribes, which was seen as a matter of prestige. Rather than being an object of faith, the Ka'ba was seen as a position of authority that built social and tribal identity. That's why almost every tribe was competing to have a share from this honor. It is a historical reality that disagreements arose between tribes; this honor was not always justly shared. In addition to the two we mentioned, other pilgrimage services were as follows: protection and security of the Ka'ba, management of the donations for the idols in the Ka'ba, and treating the pilgrims and feeding the needy ones. After the conquest of Mecca, only the two aforementioned services of providing water and maintaining the Ka'ba continued; the rest were abandoned.[18] This can be the reason why only these two were mentioned in the verse. This was the cultural background about the pilgrimage services when the verses were revealed.

Here are translations of some expressions used in the Qur'an for the Ka'ba: The first House (of Prayer) established for humankind (Al Imran 3:96); The House of God (al-Hajj 22:26); sacred temple whose vicinity was rendered secure (al-Maedah 5:97); direction to turn in the prayer (al-Baqarah 2:143); means of guidance and source of abundance (Al Imran 3:96); a resort for people, and a refuge of safety (al-Baqarah 2:125).

The Ka'ba is not a place of honor by means of which tribal egos are inflated, but it is a symbol of Divine unity; this is why it is the most sacred sanctuary of Islam. The Ka'ba is known as the House of God: the

---

17   Derveze, 7/325.

18   Abu Dawud, hadith no 4588.

most exalted of all places on earth and a symbol of faith. Other services have a secondary place vis-a-vis this primary meaning, for the Ka'ba is assumed to be a unique place where every believer leaves behind all worldly and human qualities and comes closest to the Divine. Serving such a place would not be appropriate if the servant does not have true faith. As specified in verse 17, God certainly does not want polytheists who testify to their own denial of faith with their own words, attitudes, and with their entire lives to do this service. We understand from the social background reflected by the verses that the polytheists still had expectations about this place of prestige, hoping that they could be granted a similar service in the new era. However, Islam did not approve of tribal chauvinism, and it was out of question for the highest symbol of Divine unity to be a tool for that. This verse brought an end all practices of assumed prestige from the "era of ignorance" that were not in compliance with *tawhid*: "They are those whose works have been wasted." For the polytheists had been wronging themselves "theologically" by associating partners with God and persecuting people, by way of which they would be at a loss: "And God does not guide (to truth) the wrongdoing folk."

One question that comes to mind is why it matters whether the servants are believers or not, as long as services to the pilgrims and to the Ka'ba are observed. It does not matter from a worldly perspective, but the reward from God requires an integrity of faith, intention, and practice. None of these existed with polytheists, for whom serving the pilgrims and the Ka'ba was something they demanded for ostentation, to satisfy their tribal egos, and to reinforce their rule over the land. If the intention is not for a good purpose, it destroys the action, and the evil of the action destroys faith. "Actions are by intention," said the Prophet, emphasizing this truth.

Islam binds virtuous actions to true faith and sincere intention. People's actions in this life will be judged in the hereafter with reward or punishment according to a three-dimensional assessment: faith/intention/action. The rewards in the hereafter for daily prayers or fasting performed for the sake of good health would not be the same for those done only for submitting to God's will and for seeking His good pleasure. The first ones will be told they already got their reward in this world. This is best portrayed in a *hadith* in which we find a martyr, a scholar, and a rich man in conversation with God on the day of judgment. God asks the martyr why he fought in the battlefield, the scholar why he sought knowledge, and the rich man what he did with his wealth. The martyr says he died for God, the scholar says he sought knowledge for God, and the rich man says he distributed his wealth with the poor for God. "You have lied," each of them is told: they did what they did to be called a brave warrior, a scholar, and generous.[19] Intention is the main criterion in the assessment of actions.

To the same question on why the intentions of the servants to the Ka'ba matter, Hamdi Yazır shows verse 9:18 as evidence: "Only he will maintain God's houses of worship (using them for the purposes for which they are built) who believes in God and the Last Day, and establishes the Prescribed Prayer, and pays the Prescribed Purifying Alms, and stands in awe of none but God. It is hoped that such (illustrious) persons will be among the ones guided to achieve their expectations (especially in the Hereafter)." Based on this verse, he argues that servants of a place of worship should have the basic qualifications of belief in God and belief in the Hereafter; they should observe daily prayers and alms; and they should not fear anyone except God. He says that it is not completely possible not to fear anything, but places of worship can be maintained only by those who are not deterred from serving God for the fear of anything, who always uphold God's rights when there is a conflict with their personal interests, and who do not turn away from striving on God's path even when condemned or oppressed for this."[20]

Verses 20-22 add one more quality to the Muslims who believe in God, in the Hereafter, observe daily prayers, give alms, and fear none but God: emigration. Rewards for emigration are also emphasized: "Those who believe and have emigrated (to the home of Islam in God's cause), and strive in God's cause with their wealth and persons, are greater in rank in God's sight, and those are the ones who are the triumphant. Their Lord gives them glad tidings of mercy from Him (to bring unforeseen blessings), and His being pleased with them, and of Gardens

---

19   Muslim, Imara, 152.

20   Hamdi Yazır, 4/294.

wherein is everlasting bounty for them; therein to dwell forever. Surely, with God is a tremendous reward."

At-Tawbah 9:23-24

Relations with polytheists after war

> O you who believe! Do not take your fathers and your brothers for confidants and guardians (to whom you can entrust your affairs), if they choose unbelief in preference to belief. Whoever of you takes them for confidants and guardians, those are wrongdoers (who have wronged themselves by committing a great error). (23)

> (O the Prophet!) Say (to believers): If your fathers, and your children, and your brothers and sisters, and your spouses, and your kindred and clan, and the wealth you have acquired, and the commerce you fear may slacken, and the dwellings that you love to live in, are dearer to you than God and His Messenger and striving in His cause, then wait until God brings about His decree (of retribution for not upholding the cause of faith). God does not guide the transgressing people (who prefer worldly things to Him, His Messenger and striving in His cause, to truth and true happiness in both the world and the Hereafter). (24)

The theme in these verses sound as if they have shifted from the general context of war discussed in the previous verses to how faith forges attitude. There is in fact a connection between the subjects if we consider all the verses together.

At this point, Muslims achieved things they probably wouldn't have imagined. It was a complete success story. The Ka'ba, the symbol of Divine unity, was now free; an ultimatum was given to the polytheists who did not comply with their agreement; and political authority had been established over territories including Mecca and Medina. People were able to worship in peace and securely travel for trade.

Now the Muslims were at a crossroads: how were they going to formulate their relations with the polytheists, among whom there were their closest relatives, parents, and siblings, all of whom preferred their own ways to faith? What would material and spiritual boundaries be in these relations? These verses are a warning to the Muslims on this subject matter.

According to narrations, in the days that followed the conquest of Mecca, some Muslims continued their relations with their polytheist kindred. When viewed from the polytheists' perspective, the thought of regaining their properties in the places conquered by Muslims might have played a role in that. Conversely, it is also possible that some Muslims might have contacted their relatives to reclaim their properties. Some sources note that some Muslims might have sided with their relatives when the Prophet sent expeditions to places under the polytheists' rule.

Another possible factor that can be considered in relation to these verses is *asabiyyah* in the sense of tribal partisanship that defined Arab society before Islam. What really lay under this strong social cohesion among members of a family, clan, or tribe was economic and social benefits regardless of circumstances. This type of cohesion was against the nature of society Islam prescribed. Islam did not prioritize tribal relations; it prescribed peaceful coexistence across differences of language, religion, race, tribe, or sect, and took as its basis freedom, equality, justice, meritocracy, and consultation.

So, the two verses in question make the necessary warning to Muslims and remind them where they are supposed to stand on this issue. It is stated that bonds of faith are superior to ties of kinship, even when first-degree family members are concerned. On account of different situations, several other verses that support the same meaning were revealed. Al-Mujadilah 22 is an example of these:

> You never find a people who truly believe in God and the Last Day loving towards those who oppose God and His Messenger, even if they be their (own) parents, or their children, or their brothers (and sisters), or their clan. Those (are they) in whose hearts God has inscribed faith and has strengthened them with a spirit from Him (which is the source of their spiritual vigor and intellectual enlightenment).

At this point, a question may arise in our minds: is it not a bit too heavy to refer to these Muslims as wrongdoers?

What matters about accepting Islam is that it should be absolutely free from coercion and pressure. People are free to choose their religion or unbelief. Still, Muslims are supposed to be kind to their parents, even if they are polytheists. Together with that, continuing relations with all those who approved atrocities was somewhat comparable to the situations of those who preferred oppression to faith.

In addition, it was necessary to eliminate the moral and social corruption of the pre-Islamic period. Certain boundaries needed to be drawn to let the new values of faith, morality, and justice be established in the new society. The behavioral codes of believers needed to be set. In a way, the verse portrays the new situation and cautions believers with a sharp address. After all, they may not have been completely able to rid themselves of traces of tribalism. This trait could have reappeared after the war was over. In Mecca, they had their homes, past work, and memories. Any person's heart could be inclined in that direction, but the verses commanded a new form of social behavior, and the situation of the past was over.

After these short explanations, let me answer the question we asked above: yes, the verse makes a warning with a sharp address, but it does so because a clear line needed to be drawn to separate faith and oppression. The verse mentions "preferring unbelief over faith" with reference to the position the oppressors were holding. Otherwise, choosing to believe or not depends on a person's free will after all, and the bitter fact is that those who committed oppression were those who denied faith. Therefore, unbelief and oppression had a virtually identical meaning, and every kind of struggle could continue, including military combat. Accordingly, those who did not make their side clear at such a crossroads could fail to give support when fighting back against attacks was necessary. Worldly pursuits may also deter people from the right path. It should be for this reason that verse 24 continues in the same tone.

The explanations Hamdi Yazır makes in this respect are noteworthy:

(This means) your fathers, your children, your siblings, your spouses and clan, your close relatives you spend time with, the wealth you have acquired, the commerce you fear may slacken, and the dwellings you live in—such as houses, mansions, villas, gardens, holiday resorts and all—in short, all of these family and relations, wealth and trade, living in comfort and peace are the primary reasons of amicability and warmth between groups of people. And war has a nature that separates a person from these. War separates people from their dear father, son, siblings, spouses, relatives, neighbors, and other acquaintances. War deprives people from precious commodity they earn with much labor, it stops trade and prevents enjoying comfortable beds. Therefore, war is something unpleasant, and of course it is no good to start war while living in peace. However, there is a limit to loving comfort. These are neither the ultimate goal for humanity, nor do they suffice for salvation. Loving them is good as far as they are means for righteous deeds; but they are misfortunes if they cause us to forget faith and serving God. Those who love these to the degree of preferring them to everything else can make no progress in their humanity and morality. They violate rights and law; they cause oppression and injustice. They show consent to every kind of meanness and cannot fight even in a righteous sense when necessary. Therefore, wait and see what trouble God will let befall you. Then you see whether you can be saved or not. Do you think you can? No, you can never be saved then! Know that God does not grant right guidance to a mass of transgressors who went astray. In other words, as far as you do not love God, His Messenger, and striving in God's path more than worldly love for your wealth and children, then wait for a disaster to befall you.[21]

As a final point, let us remind that verse 23 was not revealed in peace time but during war. So, the command for not taking them as "*wali*" (which we translated as "confidants and guardians") refers to Muslims having a relation with them that will have a negative impact on their relationship with God and His Messenger.

---

21   Hamdi Yazır, 4/300-301.

HYPOCRITES AND INNER THREAT

AN-NISA 4:88-89

4

HYPOCRITES AND INNER THREAT

An-Nisa 4:88-89

(O believers!) How is it with you that you are in two groups regarding the hypocrites (from Mecca, and other tribes who claim to be Muslims yet take part in the hostile machinations of their people against you), seeing that God has thrown them back (to unbelief) on account of what they have earned (by their sins)? Do you seek to guide him whom God has led astray? Whoever God has led astray, for him you cannot find a (safe) way (to follow). They yearn that you should disbelieve just as they disbelieved, so that you might be all alike. (88)

(O you who believe!) Do not, therefore, take from among them confidants and allies until they migrate (to Medina and join you) in God's cause. But if they turn away (from this call and continue their hostility against you), seize them and kill them wherever you find them; and do not take to yourselves any of them as confidant, nor as helper. (89)

The phrase above in an-Nisa 89 "kill them wherever you find them" is found in al-Baqarah 193, at-Tawbah 5, and repeated in an-Nisa 91. In previous sections, we already discussed that "them" in this phrase refers to Meccan polytheists who not only breached their treaties with the Muslims but also rejected all peace proposals and waged war against the Muslims. Let us now see who "them" refers to here in an-Nisa 89 (and 91).

According to the information related by sources in unison, "them" refers to the hypocrites, but we still need to ask which ones. Were they the hypocrites originally from Medina and who lived among the Muslims, or were they those who emigrated from Mecca and who pretended to be Muslims in Medina? A third alternative could be those who came to Medina from Mecca but then abandoned Islam, and who asked for the Prophet's permission to return to Mecca to reclaim their property in Mecca. The last two mentioned can be considered in the same category since they are from Mecca.

Scholars who commented that the verse is referring to the hypocrites in Medina relate the following as the reason for revelation. During the Battle of Uhud, some Muslims abandoned the Prophet and his army and returned to their homes. This was against the Charter of Medina, for defending the city when necessary was a shared responsibility of everyone living in Medina, including Muslims, polytheists, and Jews. After the battle, Muslims started to argue about the people who abandoned them. While some of them thought it was necessary to punish them, some of them disagreed. According to some reports, the subject of their argument was not the punishment but determining whether they were believers or not. Upon this, the verse beginning by asking why Muslims separated into two groups with different opinions about hypocrites was revealed.

However, when we consider the meaning of the verse that followed (an-Nisa 89)—"Do not, therefore, take from among them confidants and allies until they emigrate (from Mecca) in God's cause"—this affirms the second opinion that the verse is referring to the hypocrites from Mecca. Accordingly, the verse is telling about those who pretended to be Muslims when they visited Medina or those who became apostates and returned to Mecca for their properties.[1]

In order to be able to understand the original meaning of verses 90 and 91 to follow, let me briefly relate facts about the social life and groups in Medina. In terms of their faith, there were four groups of people living in Mecca and Medina: Muslims, polytheists, People

---

1   See: Ali Bulaç, *Kur'an Dersleri* [Qur'an Lessons], 2/454.

of the Book²—a majority of which were Jews—and the hypocrites. In another form of categorization, we can consider all non-Muslims in three groups: 1) enemies; 2) those under the agreement of protection; and 3) those who remained neutral. The hypocrites did not belong to any of these three groups. They were not overt enemies because they introduced themselves as Muslims and lived among Muslims. Outwardly they seemed to carry out religious observances. In the Prophet's mosque, they stood behind the noble Prophet at prayer and joined the social life like Muslims. They were not subject to the agreement of protection either. They did not clearly express their thoughts, beliefs, and lifestyles, nor did they declare that they would adopt a neutral attitude when Muslims were at war. They looked like Muslims, but what they kept inside was not consistent with their appearance. Yet, since they also showed their hypocrisy on different occasions, they were not completely indiscernible either. Hypocrites, thus, constituted a wide and unreliable group which posed a threat to Muslims—a threat no less dangerous than that posed by enemies.

The verse 89 exposes hypocrites' disbelief and true intentions: "They yearn that you should disbelieve just as they disbelieved, so that you might be all alike." Then what was supposed to be done? How should the Muslims have engaged with the hypocrites? The following verse clarified this issue: "(O you who believe!) Do not, therefore, take from among them confidants and allies until they emigrate in God's cause." Do not establish close friendship with those who went back on their promises and did not emigrate (although they could have) but instead remained with the polytheists of Mecca. Emigration from Mecca was a very critical attitude in the circumstances of that time, for it indicated a clear stance against polytheism and hypocrisy. It provided Muslims with an acid test to understand people's sincerity.

Some scholars argue that the same policy could have been followed for the hypocrites in Medina because of their similar actions and thoughts, which is an argument that should not be ignored. This argument can be exemplified by the Ifq incident when Aisha, the Prophet's wife, was slandered. In response to this incident, in chapter al-Ahzab

---

2   People of the Book, or *ahl al-kitab*, is a Qur'anic term for those tribes and nations that received a scripture. It is used mainly for Christians and Jews.

verses 33:60-61, the Qur'an gives a similarly conditional command against hypocrites if they insist on their incitement:

> (O the Prophet!) Assuredly, if the hypocrites and those in whose hearts there is a disease, and those scare-mongers in the City (given to spreading false rumors to cause disturbance in the heartland of the Islamic Community) do not desist, We will most certainly urge you against them, and then they will not be able to remain in it as your neighbors except a little while only, excluded from God's Mercy forever, and wherever they may be found, they will be seized, and killed one and all.

Back to our discussion on an-Nisa 89, the verse continues with a conditional command to kill hypocrites: "But if they turn away (from this call for faith and emigration and continue their hostility against you), seize them and kill them wherever you find them; and do not take to yourselves any of them as confidant, nor as helper."

There are a few questions to be clarified here. One is: does this pertain to all hypocrites? Given that these commands and judgments pertain to the laws of war, what would happen if the hypocrites felt frightened and took refuge in a people that has an agreement to remain neutral with the Muslims? Or after this command to kill, what would the Muslims do if the hypocrites expressed their regret and explicitly apologized? Moreover, what would be done if they did not want to fight against the Muslims, who, despite their differences of faith, were mostly from the same ethnicity? Verse 90 clarifies the issue and leaves no room for doubt.

An-Nisa 4:90

The situation of those who remain neutral

> ...except (do not fight) those who seek refuge in a people (like Huzayma) between whom and you there is a treaty (of peace or alliance), or (those who) come to you with hearts shrinking from fighting against you, as well as fighting against their own people. Had God willed, He would certainly have given them power over you and they would have fought against you. If they withdraw from

you and do not fight against you, and offer you peace, then God allows you no way (to war) against them.

As it is seen, the Qur'an makes two exceptions here. Firstly, the hypocrites taking refuge with a tribe that had a peace agreement with the Muslims was excepted. In that case, the refugees also became liable to the articles of the treaty. Secondly, those who did not wish to fight were excepted. We stated above that "these commands and judgments pertain to the laws of war." If a group is condemned to execution on account of their atrocities but they give up such acts, then the decree is suspended. If hypocrites took refuge in a people with a peace agreement with the Muslims, did this save them from the decree of execution? Yes.

This practice existed even in the pre-Islamic Arab tradition. Accordingly, if a people made an agreement of protection with another, they would also be liable to the latter's agreements with other peoples. The situation would not change even if the agreement in question was made within a time of war. Secondly, in the peace Treaty of Hudaybiyah, signed between Muslims and the Quraysh tribe of Mecca, it was stated that other tribes could be included in the agreement by siding with the Quraysh or siding with the Prophet if they wished.[3]

Thirdly, considering an-Nisa 90—"(Those who) come to you with hearts shrinking from fighting against you"—it is not acceptable to make war against those who express their unwillingness to fight against you. First of all, this would contradict the values and rules Islam prescribes. Even when taken from a rationalistic perspective, there is no point in gaining more enemies by fighting with them. The rest of the verse supports this point: "Had God willed, He would certainly have given them power over you and they would have fought against you."

In such a situation, what needs to be done is to stop war and continue life within the frame of a peace agreement. What if some who lived around Medina and who were aware of these developments continued their hypocritical acts? Sources relate that some people from the tribes of Ghatafan and Asad acted like Muslims when they came to Me-

---

3   Musnad, 4/325; Ibn Kathir, 2/354.

dina, but then they grew hostile when they returned to their own lands. The next verse covers such behaviors and the attitude to be taken.

An-Nisa 4:91

Attacking again

> (O believers!) You will find others who wish to be secure from you (by signing a treaty with you) and to be secure from their people (by breaking their treaty with you and joining them): every time they are called back to conspiracy and hostility against you, they plunge into it headlong. Hence, if they do not withdraw from you, nor offer you peace, nor restrain their hands (from hurting you), then seize them and kill them wherever you come upon them. It is against such that We have given you a clear sanction (to make war against).

The verse portrayed the typical character of the hypocrites. They wished to continue their life as safe from every kind of danger, but when some plots and plans to make war against the Muslims were revealed, their feeling of animosity was exposed; they instantly accepted a role in the plot. They seemed compliant when they were not powerful but when they thought they were powerful and could win, they plunged headfirst into troublemaking by closing their ears to suggestions of peace.

How would they be treated? Law and order in social life could not be maintained with that fickle lot. The existence of such a mutable mass likely to shoot unexpectedly any time like a mis-functional gun would threaten any society. They could not be classified as friend or foe. If one saw them as neutral, they could potentially break the agreement at any moment and join the opposing force. Even if they were an enemy, the minimum condition of maintaining peace is to remain loyal to an agreement and act in a principled fashion. The only way to maintain peace against such a fickle lot is to eliminate such distrust and potential harm. Considering the conditions of those days, the only way was war, for they had left no other humane or ethical way for diplomacy. So, the verse reflects this fact of war and depicts the context of a battlefield when it commands, "Kill them wherever you may find them."

In conclusion, according to the values of Islamic teaching, what matters is living together in peace by observing rights, justice, and fairness. A series of measures can be taken—ranging from treaty to war—against persons or groups that violate these. If words are of no use anymore and weapons have started talking, then what needs to be done is to fight for not dying. In short, the "them" mentioned in the verse "kill 'them' wherever you find them" were the fickle hypocrites, and the ground of killing them was the battlefield. So, "kill them wherever you find them" was a command strictly exclusive to the circumstances of warfare to be applied as an ultimate measure exclusively towards a very specific group.

"I am Commanded to Fight"

5

"I am Commanded to Fight"

I n many commentaries of exegesis, with reference to the verses about killing unbelievers and hypocrites, a *hadith* of the Prophet is quoted in support: "I am commanded to fight people until they say 'there is no god but God.'" As it is directly related to our subject, I would like to elaborate on this *hadith*. People find it difficult to explain this *hadith* in relation to the freedom of religion and belief in Islam. Note that forcing others to accept Islam is not allowed, and many verses and the practical life of the noble Prophet give ample evidence for this. This *hadith*, however, sounds very straightforward and seems to contradict freedom of religion. How can we then explain this?

Reported by Abdullah ibn Umar, this *hadith* is related as follows in the book of al-Bukhari:

> "I am commanded to fight against people till they say 'there is no deity but God, that Muhammad is the messenger of God,' and they establish prayer, and pay *zakat*. And if they do it, their blood and property are guaranteed protection on my behalf except when justified by law, and their affairs rest with God."

There are many points that need clarification here. Apart from the question whether this *hadith* is authenticated or not, how can its content be compatible with freedom of religion and belief? In what context did the Prophet make this statement? Who is meant by "people"? Is this a general and absolute statement to be regarded as valid for all people until the end of time, or like we see in some other *hadith*s, is there a specification about people mentioned in a particular context. Is it lawful to kill people if they are not observing the prayer and not giving the *zakat*? What could be legitimate reasons that suspend rights to life and property? What is meant by "and their affairs rest with God"? Let us explain one by one.

First of all, there is agreement on the authenticity of the first part of the *hadith*, "I am commanded to fight until they say 'there is no deity but God.'" But there are different reports about the rest of the text with some obvious contradictions. For instance, while the addition of "observing the prayer and giving the *zakat*," is found in one version, it is not found in another. There is the addition of "turning to our *qiblah* (prayer direction) and eating what we slaughter," in some narrations, while this part is missing in some others. Tracing the narrations to the Prophet's Companions, the *hadith* is quoted from the narrations of nine different people (Abdurrahman ibn Sahr ad-Dawsi, Jabir ibn Abdillah, Anas ibn Malik, Abdullah ibn Umar, Muadh ibn Jabal, Aws ibn Abi Aws, Abdullah ibn Abbas, Tarik ibn al-Ashyam, and Jarir ibn Abdillah). According to the discipline of *hadith* studies, this case is a clear example of "narration by meaning" (*riwayat bi'l ma'na*) (as opposed to narration by exact wording), since the same main meaning is narrated by different sources with certain differences in wording. If we also take into consideration expressions in some versions such as "and their affairs rest with God" which were added at the time of generations that followed the Companions (Tabi'un and their followers), it is understood that we cannot reach a sound commentary and explanation on this *hadith* without referring to classic methodology of narrative criticism.

We will not go into details like criticism of the chain of narrators, which became subject to many academic studies[1] that scrutinized each narrator. Let us instead take a look at textual differences. There are three versions reported as being from Abu Hurayrah.

The first:

---

1   See for instance, Cafer Acar, "Risalet Döneminde Savaşın Meşruiyetine İlişkin Bir Rivayet," [A Report on the Legitimacy of War During the Time of Messengership] *Iğdır Üniversitesi İlahiyat Fakültesi Dergisi*, Nisan-Ekim 2014.

"I am commanded to fight against people till they say 'there is no deity but God.' Whoever say, 'there is no deity but God,' their souls and property are guaranteed protection on my behalf except when justified by law, and (afterwards,) their affairs rest with God."[2]

This version has no details of accepting the Prophet, observing the prayer, and giving the *zakat* alms.

At the end of the second narration, the Qur'anic verses Saffat 35 and Fath 26 are added. Here is the full text of that narration:

"I am commanded to fight against people till they say 'there is no deity but God.' Whoever says, 'there is no deity but God,' their blood and property are guaranteed protection on my behalf except when justified by law, and their affairs rest with God. God mentioned a conceited people in His scripture and revealed thus: 'They feel conceit (it goes against their conceit) when it is said to them, 'there is no deity but God.' And (God) said thus: 'When those who disbelieved harbored in their hearts fierce zealotry (coming from egotism, tribalism, and feuding), the zealotry particular to the Age of Ignorance, God sent down His (gift of) inner peace and reassurance on His Messenger and on the believers, and bound them to the Word of faith, piety, and reverence for God (*taqwa*). They were most worthy of it and entitled to it.'"[3]

It is generally accepted by scholars that the verses (al-Fath 48:26) at the end of this *hadith* must be an addition by the narrator.

As for the third narration, it is the Prophet's answer to Ali ibn Abi Talib, who was going to command the army to Haybar and asked how long he was supposed to fight: "Until they bear witness as, 'There is no deity but God, and Muhammad is His Messenger.'"[4]

Lastly, in some of the narrations ascribed to Abu Hurayrah, it is said "I will continue to fight" instead of "I am ordered to..." and scholars of *hadith* also see this as a difference of expression by the narrator.

---

2   Bukhari, Jihad, 102.

3   Ibn Hibban, Sahih, 1/220.

4   Sahih al-Muslim, Iman 34.

The narration from Jabir ibn Abdillah is the same with the first *hadith* we related from Abu Hurayrah, but there is the addition of the Qur'anic verses al-Ghaashiyah 88:22-24: "You are not one to dictate (faith) to them. But whoever turns away (averse to reminder and exhortation), and disbelieves (in what is conveyed to him), God will punish him with the greatest punishment (of Hell)."[5]

As for the narration by Anas ibn Malik, one of the Companions who lived longest and was very young during the Prophet's life, it has additions we do not see in other versions. Based on verifications by scholars, the *hadith* took the following form with the additions that reflect the political upheavals of the time:

> "I am commanded to fight people until they bear witness as there
> is no deity but God, and Muhammad is His Messenger. If they bear
> witness as, there is no deity but God, and Muhammad is His Mes-
> senger, turn to our Prayer direction, eat from what we slaughtered,
> and observe our Prayer, then their blood and properties become
> forbidden (come under our protection), except when justified by
> law. What is for Muslims is for them, and what is against Muslims is
> against them."[6]

Except for the addition of "Muhammad is His Messenger," the narration from Abdullah ibn Umar is the same as that of Abu Hurayrah:

> "I have been ordered to fight against the people until they testify
> that there is no deity but God and that Muhammad is the Messenger
> of God, and until they establish the *salah* and pay the *zakat*. And if
> they do that then they will have gained protection from me for their
> lives and property, unless [justified by law], and their reckoning will
> be with God."[7]

In the narration by Muadh ibn Jabal, there is the addition of the prayer and *zakat* alms. In sum, the presence of all of these differences

---

5   Sahih al-Muslim, Iman 35; Tirmidhi, *Tafsiru'l-Qur'an*, 88.

6   Abu Dawud, Jihad, 95.

7   Bukhari, Iman 17; Muslim, Iman 36.

supports the fact that this *hadith* is an example of "narration by meaning," which is an important topic in *hadith* studies.[8]

There are also other versions stated in relation to certain historical events, which should be the reason for the additions. The most famous example but at the same time the weakest narration is the version relating the decision to go to war during the time of Caliph Abu Bakr. It concerned the people who said they would observe the prescribed prayers but stop giving the *zakat* alms after the Prophet's demise. Prior to the battles recorded in history as the Ridda Wars, Umar ibn al-Khattab objected to this decision by Abu Bakr and asked on what basis he was waging war against people who observed the prayer. Abu Bakr answered that the Messenger of God had stated, "I am commanded to fight against the people until they testify that there is no deity but God and that Muhammad is the Messenger of God, and until they establish the prayer and pay the (alms of) *zakat*." Then Abu Bakr continued, saying, "I swear by God, even if it was a young goat they would give to the Messenger of God but not to us, I will fight them."

This narration in Bazzar's *musnad*, *Al-Bahru'z Zahhar*, was reported by Anas ibn Malik and is a very famous one, but in its different versions in other works like Hakim's *Mustadrak* and Bayhaqi's *Sunan*, there is no reference to the *hadith* "I am commanded to fight..."

There are other narrations for explaining the *hadith*. For example, Abdullah ibn Amr ibn al-As was assigned as governor to Kufa during the caliphate of Umar ibn al-Khattab. At one point, complaints about incidents of depravity being on the rise in the city started reaching Caliph Umar. He asked the governor why he did not take measures. The governor answered by mentioning the *hadith* "I am commanded to fight people until they say there is no deity but God,"[9] implying that those incidents did not cause any harm in the public order, which he understood, as it were, within the framework of this *hadith*.

Having related these general facts about the narration of the *hadith*, let us evaluate it in terms of our main subject:

8   Ibn Maja, Muqaddima, 9.

9   Tabarani, Awsat, 7/6966; Fayda, Mustafa, "Abdullah ibn Amr b. al-As", *DIA*, Istanbul 1988.

   In spite of all those different versions, there is a general agreement that this *hadith* is authenticated in terms of the chain of narration.

   With regards to textual criticism (a main component of *hadith* studies), it was not seriously questioned to what degree this *hadith* complied with the general values of Islam. Thus, we can only assume that such a textual criticism was not seen as necessary given the circumstances of that era; the *hadith* was accepted as it was. We are now looking at the text from the perspective of the twenty-first century, at a time when we talk about concepts like freedom of belief, expression, and the like. If we consider that such freedoms became established and systemized concepts to be included in international treaties only after the nineteenth century, expecting the same conceptualization from the early scholars would not be fair. We, on the other hand, are able to look back into history and classify events based on modern viewpoints. Yet we also know that the Qur'an makes frequent emphasis of these concepts. For example: "Then, whoever wills (to believe), let him believe; and whoever wills (to disbelieve), let him disbelieve" (al-Kahf 18:29). Or there are many verses that emphasize diversity of belief such as: "If God had so willed, He would surely have made them (all people) a single community" (ash-Shura 42:8).

   The narrations we quoted above have outward contradictions with such verses. This may not have been studied as a serious issue in the past, but today it is possible to eliminate such contradictions and make interpretations and commentaries on freedoms in compliance with the main purposes of the Qur'an; not that it merely can be done, but it must be done. This task is of utmost importance both in terms of explaining seeming contradictions and understanding such narrations in accordance with purposes of the Qur'an. The academic Izzat Darwaza's commentary in this respect is a conclusion to be drawn by anyone who views the issue thus. While interpreting verses at-Tawbah 4 and 5 he said: "Let us point out that these *hadith*s we mentioned create a problem in relation to the verses we are interpreting. The Messenger of God states that he was commanded to fight people until they said there is no deity but God. When these *hadith*s are taken by their face value, there will be contradiction with many judgments of the Qur'an. Actually, the Qur'an explicitly states that there is no coercion in accepting religion and that God does not forbid Muslims from having good relations with people who do not fight against them. Together with that, if there is a case of warfare against Muslims, the Qur'an commands them to defend themselves. Here, we assert that it is not possible for the Messenger of God to contradict established Qur'anic principles. Sound reports about both his life practices and those of the Four Caliphs relate that they did not fight against anyone except for those who showed hostility and aggression against Muslims from the outset or by breaching their peace treaty. Then it is understood that the two *hadith* in question are related to their relevant circumstances."[10]

What is meant by "people" in the *hadith* is, as many scholars have stated, Arab polytheists—namely those who were at war against the Muslims. This shows us that those actually mentioned are enemies in an ongoing war. Otherwise, this judgment is not valid for normal circumstances during a valid agreement of peace, protection, or impartiality.

The main reason for additions like "until they turn to our prayer direction and eat from what we sacrifice..." was the fact that the *hadith* was employed in history in connection to certain historical events. As these additions were expressions used for the sake of letting the *hadith* make better sense in a certain situation, they take the *hadith* out of their original context, maybe too far from what the Prophet intended to mean. For instance, this *hadith* is shown as a legal basis by those jurists who argue that not observing daily prayers requires punishment.

There is a very important detail in terms of Arabic grammar here, which urgently needs to be highlighted. The original wording of the *hadith* says, "*uqaatila*," which indicates fighting between two or more groups. Especially when those who are not knowledgeable about the rules of classic Arabic—say, if they are native speakers of everyday language—see this word, they often think "killing," which is of the same root. However, "*uqaatila*" does not mean killing, but it means fighting/making war. Killing is among the possible outcomes of war, of course, but being commanded to fight does not mean to start war without observing any law or principles whatsoever; likewise, it does not mean killing everybody without recognizing any law. Other Qur'anic verses

10   Derveze, et-Tefsiru'l-Hadis, 7/314.

related to this subject and practices of the Prophet do not support such an approach.

This important detail mostly escapes attention. Actually, it is my belief that contemporary radicals are aware of this detail. Because we know that some of the persons behind such movements have expertise in Islamic teachings, at least to some degree. However, since this does not suit their purposes, they rather take lawlessness, anarchy, and violence as their basis, and they interpret verses and *hadiths* as they wish and commit acts accordingly. Otherwise, from a perspective of the general purposes of the Qur'an and Islam, it is not possible to find an acceptable basis for their interpretation. I am of the opinion that *being commanded to fight* means showing the resolution to do so if necessary. If this resolution is shown, things can develop in a favorable way and the problem can probably be solved without any dying or killing. There are so many examples of that in the history of Islam.

In sum, on account of the overgeneralized meaning, this *hadith* was employed in different occasions throughout history in a way that conflicts with Islamic values, freedom of religion being the first. While the word "people" mentioned in the *hadith* refers to the hostile Arab polytheists at the time of the Prophet, many who strayed from justice for their personal political interests took it to mean "opposition" and justified their oppression. The *hadith* was approached only by taking its text into consideration, and it was detached from its historical context—and thus from its original meaning. They tried to tackle problems by making additions, thus relating the *hadith* to the problems that arose in their time. Be it a verse added for the sake of its relation to the subject, a sentence mistakenly ascribed to the Prophet, or individuals' own comments, the result does not change. Even if some of these were done with good intentions, the *hadith* was consequently detached from its original meaning.

Today, not only ordinary people but even people with some degree of familiarity with Islamic subjects are prone to understand this *hadith* in a way that contradicts freedom of religion. The Prophet was told in the Qur'an that he was "not one to dictate (faith) to them" (al-Ghaashiyah 88:22). If the Prophet was commanded not to force people into faith, how can it be possible for him to literally mean that he would fight against people until they became Muslim? Unfortunately, there exists a mentality that does not see the conflict between the two statements today.

In my opinion, one factor that played a major role in this misunderstanding were the narrations claiming that Caliph Abu Bakr used this *hadith* as a proof to suppress those who refused to pay *zakat* as tax, which means they refused to recognize state authority. Both attitudes taken by the Prophet and Caliph Abu Bakr were political ones necessitated by circumstances of warfare. The *zakat* alms and the prayer in these narrations—if they are not added by the narrators—are expressions of secondary importance that serve to describe Muslim society as opposed to hostile Arab polytheists. In many other verses, observances like the prayer and *zakat*, which are public symbols of Islam, are emphasized when a Muslim society is portrayed. In short, the main idea in the *hadith* is not the prayer and alms of *zakat*, but the hostile attitude of the people who prepared for war. Together with this, when viewed from the perspective of *hadith* narration criticism, it can be argued that these statements are possibly additions by narrators.

CONCLUSION

CONCLUSION

The Qur'an was revealed over a timeline of more than two decades, in the context of certain specific situations early Muslims faced. In the person of the Prophet and other first-generation Muslims, the Qur'an conveys general teachings and guidelines to be followed by all Muslims. The first-hand addressees were able to understand the message of the scripture without needing much scholarly explanation, thanks to the direct guidance of the noble Prophet. Early generations were able to make right sense of verses by establishing proper connection between the phenomenon and norm. There was no better way to understand how Qur'anic teachings apply to real life practice.

Achieving this called for mental effort and, of course, methodology. Right after the Prophet passed away, his Companions and the following two generations set about many diligent scholarly studies. They established and developed the methodology of essential Islamic disciplines. As for historical studies, they aimed to provide authenticated reference for the essential disciplines by recording the words and practices of the Prophet and his Companions.

The point I am insistently trying to emphasize is that Qur'anic verses are best understood when studied in the context of the events experienced at the time of revelation between the years 610-632 CE, from the advent of Islam until the Prophet's demise. Looking at the verses of jihad from this perspective, for instance, we realize that they were revealed in relation to the events of the time to guide Muslims with practical solutions to real problems.

I personally believe using phrases like "war or peace in international relations according to Islam" is not right. "In Islam...," "according to Islam...," or other similar phrases dominate the discussion and make the audience assume what follows these phrases to be direct commandments from God or the Prophet. However, what follows are usually conclusions drawn from verses as understood by the speaker or the writer. In other words, they reflect personal understandings, thoughts, comments, and interpretations. In this respect, it is very important to choose our words accordingly, so that our audience or readers understand the commentary cited may not be absolute but is one among perhaps many commentaries on Islamic essentials. Writers and speakers do not necessarily intend to monopolize ideas, but such phrases make it sound otherwise.

Islam is the title for a religion, which is a body of teachings to be followed by Muslims until the end of the world. Accordingly, Islam gives us its universal principles and values from which we can derive guidance to respond to different situations. Based on these values, it is us, as humans, who are supposed to develop theories and doctrines and implement them in our lives, especially in fields as dynamic as international relations that are constantly changing according to conditions and depending on the will of people and their political representatives. One should not view Islam and the Qur'an as a theory, doctrine, or a book of law; likewise, one should not view Prophet as a person put in charge to enforce such a doctrine or book of law. "Is war or peace essential in international relations in the light of Islamic values?" would be a more correct way to address the matter.

"International relations" evolved as a concept after the emergence of modern states. Considering the Hijaz peninsula when the Qur'an was revealed, there was neither a state nor a governmental structure in the contemporary sense, nor was there a theoretical frame for such relations. To put it as fairly as possible, it is only possible to talk about "war and peace" concerning those days. But in today's world, there are countless theories with regards to international relations. Given that there are jihad verses in the Qur'an, is it not possible for a theory of war or peace to be based on Qur'anic verses?

It is surely possible. However, this is possible with the condition of not forgetting the relation between phenomenon and the norm, or realpolitik and ideal politics, as we expressed before. Phenomenon or realpolitik pertain to the events that occurred during the process of revelation and the verses that brought a solution to them; whereas ideal politics pertain to values and principles to be drawn as a result of a holistic perspective on the Qur'an, including the verses of jihad.

To give a particular example, the first part of verse 191 of al-Baqarah states "kill them wherever you may come upon them"; this is in reference to the Meccan polytheists and pertains to the realpolitik. Meanwhile, "*Fitnah* (namely persecuting and torturing people because of their beliefs) is worse than killing" in the same verse pertains to ideal politics from which we can draw the principle of freedom of religion and belief.

Thus, our discussion comes to the real reason lying behind the manifesto I mentioned in the beginning of this book that demands the abrogation of Qur'anic verses involving violence. Here, I would like to point out with special emphasis that in the historical process, the task of drawing norm from phenomena and noticing the nuance between realpolitik and ideal politics, was not realized within the frame we try to present here. The reasons for this merit a separate work that can discuss the matter under the headings of epistemology and methodology.

In conclusion, I would like to reiterate that it is wrong to sloganize the issue by making claims like, "Islam is a religion of war" or "Islam is a religion of peace." I believe that such reductionist and non-scholarly discourses place a barrier before understanding Islam. War-or-peace is a political issue that pertains to international relationships. Those who will make such decisions are political authorities according to the circumstances of their time. Giving priority to peace is an ideal, for sure; however, war is a reality depending on the conditions of the time. A balanced pro-peace policy where war is recognized as an undesired but an inevitable option better expresses Islamic values. Rather than describing Islam with reference to war or peace, it will be more proper to define it as a religion of justice based on mercy and compassion. Islam is the title for a religion that commands having compassion and mercy for the whole of creation, but without neglecting justice at the same time. As mentioned before, Islam takes as basis justice in social relations, moderation and integrity in religious feelings, and compassion and mercy in relations with the whole of creation.

To conclude, a civilization is built on concepts; if you wish, you can read this statement the other way round and say that it is concepts that build a civilization.

Concepts are like living organisms. Depending on unfolding events, the meaning they contain narrows, expands, changes, or transforms. The Qur'an built its own concepts, and jihad is among them. Conditions that changed along the many centuries since the advent of Islam have narrowed, expanded, changed, and transformed jihad's frame of meaning. Today, what falls to Muslims is bringing back jihad to its right Qur'anic ground and restoring its real meaning.

BIBLIOGRAPHY

Abdulbaki, M. Fuad, *al-Mu'jamu'l-Mufahras li Alfazi'l-Qur'ani'l-Karim*, Istanbul, 1984.

Abdulfattah al-Kadi, *al-Asbab al-Nuzul*, Ankara, 2016.

Ahmad b. Hanbal, *al-Musnad*, Beirut, 1985.

Ahmed, Akbar, Grian Forst, *After Terror*, USA, 2005.

Aksu, Ali, *"Asr-ı Saadet, Hulefa-i Raşidin ve Emeviler Döneminde Fikir Hürriyeti*," *CÜİFD*, vol. v, no. 2, Sivas, 2001.

Aktan, Hamza, *"Kazf"* *DİA*, Ankara, 2002.

Aktan, Hamza, *"Kur'an ve Sünnet Işığında Terör ve İntihar Eylemleri*," *Yeni Ümit*, no. 63, Istanbul, 2004.

Aktan, Hamza, *İslam Hukukunun Dinamizmi*, Erzurum, 1991.

Aliyyu'l-Kari, Nuruddin Ali b. Muhammad, *al-Asraru'l- Marfûa fi'l-Ahbari'l-Mawdua*, Beirut, 1971.

Alusi, *Ruhu'l-Maani fi Tafsiri'l-Qur'ani'l-Azim wa's-Sab'il-Masani*, Daru ihyai'tturasi'l-arabi, Beirut, Ts.

Altındaş, Ramazan, "Maturidi Kelam Sisteminde Akıl-Nakil İlişkisi," *Marife*, year 5, Vol. 3, Winter 2005.

Altuntaş, Halil, *İslam'da Din Hürriyeti ve Temelleri*, Ankara, 2000.

Apaydın, H. Yunus, "İçtihad", *DİA*, Istanbul, 2000.

Arı, M. Salih, *Hz. Ebu Bekir ve Ridde Savaşları*, Istanbul, 1995.

Armağan, Servet, *İslam Hukukunda Temel Haklar ve Hürriyetler*, Ankara, 1992.

Arsal, Sadri Maksudi, *Hukukun Umumi Esasları Hukukun Pozitif Felsefesi*, Ankara, 1937.

Asım Efendi, *Kamus Tercemesi*, s.l., n.d.

Avva, Muhammed Selim, *Fi Usuli'n-Nizami'l-Jinaiyyi'l-Islami*, Cairo, 1983.

Apak, Adem, *Kur'an'ın Geliş Ortamında Arap Toplumu*, Istanbul, 2017

Aydın, Mehmet, *Güncel Dini Meseleler İstişare Toplantısı*, Istanbul, 2002.

Ateş, Ali Osman, *İslam'a Göre Cahiliye ve Ehli Kitap Örf ve Adetleri*, Istanbul, 2014.

Ateş, Süleyman, *Yüce Kur'an'ın Çağdaş Tefsiri*, Istanbul, 1989.

Bardakoğlu, Ali, *Güncel Dini Meseleler İstişare Toplantısı*, Ankara, 2004

Bardakoğlu, Ali, *İslam Işığında Müslümanlığımızla Yüzleşme*, Kuramer, 2016.

Bayraktar, Mehmet, *İslam'da Düşünce Özgürlüğü*, Ankara, 1995.

Belazuri, *Futuhu'l-Buldan*, trans. by Mustafa Fayda, Ankara, 2002.

Bediüzzaman, Said Nursi, *Münazarat*, Istanbul, 1998.

Bilmen, Ömer Nasuhi, *Hukuk-i Islamiyye ve Istılahat-ı Fikhiyye Kamusu*, Istanbul, 1967.

Bukhari, Abu Abdillah Muhammad b. Ismail, *as-Sahih*, Riyadh, 2000.

Bulaç, Ali, *Kur'an Dersleri*, Istanbul, 2016.

Bulaç, Ali, "Cihad", *Yeni Ümit*, no. 63, Istanbul, 2004.

Bulut, Mehmet, "Tebliğ", İİİGYA, Istanbul, 1997.

Al-Buti, Said Ramazan, *Fıqhu's Sirat*, Istanbul, 1986.

Bury, John, *Düşünce Özgürlüğünün Tarihi*, trans. by Durul Bartu, Istanbul, 1978.

140   The Ultimatum

Cole, Juan, *Muhammad: Prophet of Peace Amid the Clash of Empires*, New York, 2013.
Considine, Craig, *The Humanity of Muhammad: A Christian Perspective*, Clifton: NJ, 2020.
Cabiri, Muhammad Abid, *Kur'an'a Giriş*, Istanbul, 2013.
Çağrıcı, Mustafa, "Hürriyet", *DİA*, Istanbul, 1998.
Dalgın, Nihat, *Gündemdeki Tartışmalı Dini Konular*, Istanbul, 2004.
Dalgın, Nihat, *"Temel Kaynaklar Çerçevesinde Dinden Dönme ve İnanç Özgürlüğü," Makâlât*, no. 1, Konya 1991.
Derveze, İzzet, *et-Tefsirül Hadis*, Istanbul, 2014.
Derveze, İzzet, *Kur'an'a Göre Hz. Muhammed'in Hayatı*, Istanbul, 2015.
Dorman, Emre, *İslam Ne Değildir*, Istanbul, 2018.
Abu Dawud, Suleyman b. al-Ash'as, *as-Sunan*, Riyadh, 2000.
Ebu Süleyman, Ahmet, *İslam'ın Uluslararası İlişkiler Kuramı*, trans. into Turkish by Fehmi Koru, Ankara,1985.
Ebu Zehra, Muhammed, *İslam Hukuk Metodolojisi*, trans. into Turkish by A. Kadir Şener, Ankara, 1990.
Ebu Zehra, Muhammed, *İslam'da Savaş Kavramı*, trans. into Turkish by Cemal Karaağaçlı, Istanbul, 1985.
Ecer, A. Vehbi, *"Mekke'nin Fethi ve Sonuçları," İslam'da İnsan Modeli ve Hz. Peygamber* Örneği, Ankara, 1995.
Elmalılı, M. Hamdi Yazır, *Hak Dini Kur'an Dili*, Istanbul, 1979.
Erdal, Mesud, *Kur'an'da Fitne Kavramı* Üzerine *Düşünceler*, DÜİFD, Diyarbakır 1999.
Eren, Şadi, *Cihad ve Savaş*, Istanbul, 1996.
Es'ad, Mahmud, *İslam Tarihi*, simplified by. A. Lütfi Kazancı-Osman Kazancı, Istanbul, 1983.
Erdoğan, Mehmet, *İslâm Hukukunda Ahkamın Değişmesi*, Istanbul, 1990.
Esed, Muhammed, *Kur'an Mesajı, Meal-Tefsir*, Trans. by Cahit Koytak, Ahmet Ertürk, Istanbul, 1999.
Fayda, Mustafa, *Hz. Ömer Zamanında Gayr-ı Müslimler*, Istanbul, 1989.
Fazlur Rahman, *İslami Yenilenme, Makaleler* II. Trans. by Adil Çiftci, Ankara, 2000.
Görmez, Mehmet, *Güncel Dini Meseleler İstişare Toplantısı*, Ankara, 2004.
Gülen, Fethullah, "Zeki Sarıtoprak ve Ali Ünal ile Röportaj", *The Muslim World*, y. 95, no. 3.
——, *İ'la-yı Kelimetullah veya Cihad*, İzmir, 1997.
——, *İrşad Ekseni*, Izmir, 2001.
Güneş, Ahmet, *İslam Kamu Hukukunda Fikir ve* İnanç *Hürriyeti*, unpublished PhD thesis, Erzurum, 2003.
Hamidullah, Muhammed, *"Hudeybiye Anlaşması"*, *DİA*, Istanbul, 1998.
——, *"İslam'da Gayr-i Müslimlerin Durumu"*, *İslam Anayasa Hukuku*, trans. by Mustafa Sabri Küçükkaşçı, edited by Vecdi Akyüz, Istanbul, 1995.
——, *Hazreti Peygamberin Savaşları*, Istanbul, 1981.
——, *İslam Peygamberi*, trans. by Salih Tuğ, Istanbul, 1993.

———, İslam'da *Devlet* İdaresi, trans. by Kemal Kuşcu, Ankara, 1979.

———, *Majmuatu'l Wasaiki's-Siyasiyya li'l-Ahdi'in Nabawiyya wa'l-Hilafe-ti'r-Rashidati*, Beirut, 1987.

Hashim, Jamil, "as-Salam fi'l-Islam", *Risaletu'l İslamiyye*, pp. 63-64.

Hilafeti'r-Raşideti, Beirut 1987.

Haylamaz, Reşit, *Efendimiz*, Izmir, 2006.

Haythami, Nuraddin b. Ali Abi Bakr, *Majmau'z-Zawaid wa Manbau'l Fawaid*, Beirut, 1967.

Ibn Abdil Barr, Abu Omar Yusuf b Abdullah al-Kurtubi, *ad-Durar fi Ihtisa-ri'l-Maghazi wa's-Siyar*, Morocco, 1980.

Ibn Arabi, Abu Bakr Muhammad b. Abdillah b. Muhammad al-Maafiri, *Ahka-mu'l Kur'an*, n.d.

Ibn Hajar, Shihabuddin Ahmad b. Ali al-Asqalani, *Fathu'l Bari*, Beirut, 1993.

Ibn Hisham, *as-Siratu'n-Nabawiyya*, s.l. n.d.

Ibn Humam, Kamaluddin Muhammad b. Abdulwahid, *Sharhu Fathi'l Qadir*, Cairo, 1970.

Ibn Kathir, *Abu Fida Ismail ibn Omer, Tafsiru'l Qur'ani'l-Azim*, Riyadh, 1977.

Ibn Kayyim al-Jawziyya, *Ahkamu ahl al-Dhimmah*, annotated bu Subhi Salih, Damascus, 1961.

Ibn Sa'd, Muhammad b. Sa'd, *at-Tabakatu'l-Kubra*, Beirut, n.d.

Ibn Majah, Ebu Abdillah Muhammad b. Yazid, *as-Sunan*, Riyadh, 2000.

Jassas, Abu Bakr Ahmad b. Ali ar-Razi, *Ahkamu'l Qur'an*, Beirut, n.d.

Kamali, Mohammad Hashim, *Shari'ah Law: An Introduction*, New York, 2008.

Kapani, Münci, *Kamu Hürriyetleri*, Ankara, 1993.

Karadavi, Yusuf, *Öncelikler Fıkhı*, trans. into Turkish Abdullah Kahraman, Istanbul, 2017.

Karafi, Abu'l Abbas Ahmad, *al-Furuk*, Beirut, 1418/1988.

———, *al-Ihkam fi Tamyizi'l-Ahkam ani'l-Ahkam*, Beirut, 1995.

Kasani, Alauddin Abu Bakr b. Masud, *Badaiu's-Sanai' fi Tartibi'sh-Sharai'*, Beirut, 1986.

Kırbaşoğlu, Hayri "İslam'a Yamanan Sanal Şiddet: Recm ve İrtidat Meselesi" *İslamiyat Dergisi*, vol. v, no. 1, Ankara, 2002.

Kurucan, Ahmet, *Altın Kuşak*, Izmir, 1999.

———, "Yürürlükte Olmayan Hukuk Olmaz…" https://www.tr724.com/yurur-lukte-olmayan-hukuk-olmaz/

Komisyon, *Kur'an Yolu Türkçe Meal ve Tefsir*, Ankara, 2006.

Köse, Feyza Betül, *Medine'de Sosyal Hayat – Dört Halife Dönemi*, Istanbul, 2016.

Malik b. Anas, *Muvatta'*, s.l. 1951.

Mawardi, Ali b. Muhammad b. Habib, *Kitabu Kitali ahli'l-Baghy mina'l-Ha-vi'l-Kabir*, annotated by Ibrahim b. Ali Sandukci, Cairo, 1987.

Ma'luf, Levis, *al-Munjid fi'l Luga*, Tehran, 1963.

Mawdudi, Abu'l-Ala, *Hilafet ve Saltanat*, trans. by Ali Genceli, Istanbul, 1980.

Mukatil b. Suleyman, *at-Tafsiru'l Kabir*, Beirut, 2002.

Muhammed Tahir b. Aşur, *İslam Hukuk Felsefesi* trans. by V. Akyüz, M. Erdoğan, Istanbul, 1988.

Muhammad Abid al-Jabiri, Hasan Hanafi, *Doğu-Batı Tartışmaları*, trans. by Muhammed Coşkun, Istanbul, 2018.

Muslim, Abu Husayn Muslim b. Hajjaj, *as-Sahih*, Riyadh, 2000.

Nargül, Veysel, *Kur'an ve Hz. Peygamberin Uygulamaları Işığında Cihad*, unpublished PhD thesis, Erzurum, 2005.

Nasai, Abu Abdirrahman b. Ash'as, *as-Sunan*, Riyadh, 2000.

Osman, Abdulkerim, İslam'da *Fikir ve* İnanç *Hürriyeti*, trans. by Ramazan Nazlı, Istanbul, n.d.

Öktem, M. Niyazi, Özgürlük *Sorunu ve Hukuk*, Istanbul, 1977.

Önkal, Ahmet, *Rasulullah'ın* İslam'a *Da'vet Metodu*, Konya 1987.

Özsoy, Ömer, *Sünnetullah: Bir Kur'an İfadesinin Kavramsallaşması*, Ankara, 1994

Öztürk, Mustafa, *Kur'an-ı Kerim Meali Anlam ve Yorum Merkezli Çeviri*, Ankara, 2016.

——, *İlahi Hitabın Tefsiri*, Ankara, 2020.

Öz, Mustafa, *İslam'da İnanç İbadet ve Günlük Yaşayış Ansiklopedisi*, "Cihad", Istanbul, 1997.

Razi, Fahruddin ar-, *Tefsir-i Kebir (Mefatihu'l-Gayb)*, trans. into Turkish by S.Yıldırım, L.Cebeci, S.Kılıç, C.S. Doğru, Ankara, 1989.

——, *at-Tafsiru'l-Kabir (Mafatihu'l-Ghayb)*, n.d.

Ridha, Rashid,*Tafsiru'l-Manar*, Beirut, 1973.

Saka, Şevki, *Kur'an-ı Kerim'in Davet Metodu*, Istanbul, n.d.

Sabuni, Muhammed Ali, *Ravaiu'l Beyan Tefsiru'l Ayati'l Ahkam*, Istanbul, n.d.

——, *Safwatu't-Tafasir*, trans. by S. Gümüş, N.Yılmaz, Istanbul, 1990.

Şafak, Ali, "İnsan Haklarına Mukayeseli Hukuk Açısından Kısa Bir Bakış", *Diyanet İlmi Dergisi*, v. XXVIII, no. I, Ankara 1992.

Sarahsi, Muhammad b. Ahmad, *al-Mabsut*, Istanbul, 1983.

——, *Sharhu Kitabi's-Siyari'l-Kabir*, Beirut 1997, trans. by: M. Erdoğan, Istanbul, 1991.

Schacht, Joseph, İslam *Hukukuna Giriş*, trans. by Mehmet Dağ-Abdulkadir Şener, Ankara, 1977.

Selahattin, Muhammed, Özgürlük *Arayışı ve İslam*, trans. by N. Ahmet Asrar, Istanbul, 1989.

Shatibi, Ibrahim b. Musa b. Muhammad, *al-Muwafakat fi Usuli'sh-Shari'a*.

Soroush, Abdolkarim, *Reason, Freedom, and Democracy in Islam*, London 1999.

Suyuti, Abu'l-Fazl Jalaluddin Abdurrahman b. Abi Bakr b. Muhammad al-Hudayri as-, *al-Itkan fi Ulumi'l Qur'an*, n.d.

Tabari, Muhammad b. Jarir, *Jamiu'l Bayan an Ta'wili Ayi'l Qur'an*, Beirut, 2000.

Tirmidhi, Abu Isa Muhammad b. Isa, *al-Jamiu's-Sahih*, Riyadh, 2000.

Topaloğlu, Bekir, "Cihad", DİA, Istanbul, 1993.

Türköne, Mümtaz'er, İslam *ve Şiddet*, Istanbul, 2007.

Udah, Abdulkadir, *at-Tashriu'l-Jinai al-Islami Mukaranan bi'l-Kanuni'l-Vad'i*, Beirut n.d.

Umara, Muhammad, *al-Islam wa Hukuku'l-Insan*, Kuwait, 1985.

Ünal, Ali, *Kur'an-ı Kerim ve Açıklamalı Meali*, Istanbul, 2006.

Waqidi, Muhammad b. Omar, *Kitabu'l-Maghazi*, Oxford, 1966.

——, *Kitabu'r-Ridda wa Nabzatun min Futuhi'l-Iraq*, annotated by Babenki Bor, Paris, 1989.

Yavuz, Yunus Vehbi, İslam'da *Düşünce ve İnanç Özgürlüğü*, Istanbul, 1994.

Yıldırım, Suat, *Kur'an-ı Hâkim ve Açıklamalı Meali*, New Jersey, 2018.

Yılmaz, M. Kazım, "İnsan Hakları Üzerine Bazı Tahliller", *Diyanet İlmi Dergisi*, vol. 28, no. I, Ankara 1992.

Yiğit, Yaşar, "İnanç ve Düşünce Özgürlüğü Perspektifinden İrtidat Suç ve Cezasına Bakış", *İslamiyat*, vol. 2, no. 2, Ankara 1999.

Zeydan, Abdülkerim, *İslam Şeriatında Fert ve Devlet*, trans. by O. Zeki Soyyiğit, Istanbul, 1969.

Zuhayli, Vehbi, *"İslam Dünyasında İctihad Tartışmaları"*, Uluslararası İslam Düşüncesi Konferansı, Istanbul, 1997.

INDEX